MASTER YOUTUBE

FROM ZERO TO MILLIONS OF SUBSCRIBERS

DAVID SANDUA

Master YouTube: From Zero to Millions of Subscribers.
© David Sandua 2024. All rights reserved.
Electronic and paperback edition.

*"I don't care about the money.
I care about the people."*

MrBeast (Jimmy Donaldson)

INDEX

I. INTRODUCTION 10
   OVERVIEW OF YOUTUBE AS A PLATFORM 11
   IMPORTANCE OF SUBSCRIBER COUNT 12
   PURPOSE OF THE ESSAY 14

II. UNDERSTANDING YOUTUBE 16
   HISTORY AND EVOLUTION OF YOUTUBE 17
   YOUTUBE'S ROLE IN DIGITAL MEDIA 18
   DEMOGRAPHICS OF YOUTUBE USERS 20

III. CREATING A YOUTUBE CHANNEL 22
   CHOOSING A NICHE 23
   SETTING UP YOUR CHANNEL 25
   CRAFTING A CHANNEL DESCRIPTION 26

IV. DEVELOPING A CONTENT STRATEGY 29
   IDENTIFYING TARGET AUDIENCE 30
   CONTENT TYPES AND FORMATS 31
   PLANNING A CONTENT CALENDAR 33

V. BUILDING A PERSONAL BRAND 36
   CREATING A UNIQUE IDENTITY 37
   DESIGNING CHANNEL ART AND LOGO 38
   ESTABLISHING A CONSISTENT VOICE 40

VI. VIDEO PRODUCTION BASICS 42
   EQUIPMENT AND SOFTWARE NEEDS 43
   SCRIPTING AND STORYBOARDING 46
   FILMING TECHNIQUES 47

VII. EDITING YOUR VIDEOS 50
   CHOOSING EDITING SOFTWARE 51
   EDITING STYLES AND TECHNIQUES 52
   ADDING MUSIC AND SOUND EFFECTS 54

VIII. THUMBNAILS AND TITLES 56
   IMPORTANCE OF THUMBNAILS 57
   CREATING CLICK-WORTHY TITLES 58
   A/B TESTING THUMBNAILS AND TITLES 60

IX. UNDERSTANDING YOUTUBE ALGORITHMS 62
   HOW THE ALGORITHM WORKS 63
   FACTORS AFFECTING VIDEO RANKING 64
   STRATEGIES TO WORK WITH THE ALGORITHM 66

X. OPTIMIZING VIDEO DESCRIPTIONS 69
   IMPORTANCE OF DESCRIPTIONS 70
   KEYWORD RESEARCH AND USAGE 71
   CALLS TO ACTION IN DESCRIPTIONS 73

XI. ENGAGING WITH YOUR AUDIENCE 75
   RESPONDING TO COMMENTS 76
   CREATING COMMUNITY POSTS 77
   HOSTING LIVE Q&A SESSIONS 79

XII. PROMOTING YOUR VIDEOS 81
- SOCIAL MEDIA MARKETING STRATEGIES 82
- COLLABORATIONS WITH OTHER CREATORS 84
- PAID ADVERTISING OPTIONS 85

XIII. ANALYZING VIDEO PERFORMANCE 87
- USING YOUTUBE ANALYTICS 88
- KEY METRICS TO TRACK 90
- ADJUSTING STRATEGIES BASED ON DATA 91

XIV. MONETIZATION OPTIONS 94
- YOUTUBE PARTNER PROGRAM 95
- SPONSORSHIPS AND BRAND DEALS 97
- MERCHANDISING AND AFFILIATE MARKETING 98

XV. BUILDING A COMMUNITY 101
- CREATING A LOYAL FANBASE 102
- ENGAGING WITH FANS OFF-PLATFORM 104
- HOSTING EVENTS AND MEETUPS 105

XVI. STAYING CONSISTENT 107
- IMPORTANCE OF REGULAR UPLOADS 108
- CREATING A SUSTAINABLE SCHEDULE 110
- BALANCING QUALITY AND QUANTITY 112

XVII. ADAPTING TO TRENDS 114
- IDENTIFYING CURRENT TRENDS 115
- INTEGRATING TRENDS INTO CONTENT 116
- STAYING RELEVANT IN A CHANGING LANDSCAPE 118

XVIII. HANDLING CRITICISM AND NEGATIVITY 120
- RESPONDING TO NEGATIVE COMMENTS 121
- LEARNING FROM CRITICISM 122
- MAINTAINING MENTAL WELL-BEING 124

XIX. LEGAL AND COPYRIGHT CONSIDERATIONS 126
- UNDERSTANDING COPYRIGHT LAWS 127
- FAIR USE AND CONTENT CREATION 128
- PROTECTING YOUR CONTENT 130

XX. NETWORKING WITH OTHER CREATORS 133
- BUILDING RELATIONSHIPS IN THE COMMUNITY 134
- ATTENDING CONFERENCES AND EVENTS 135
- COLLABORATIVE CONTENT CREATION 137

XXI. SCALING YOUR CHANNEL 139
- STRATEGIES FOR GROWTH 140
- EXPANDING CONTENT OFFERINGS 142
- DIVERSIFYING PLATFORMS 143

XXII. CASE STUDIES OF SUCCESSFUL CREATORS 146
- ANALYZING TOP YOUTUBERS 147
- LESSONS LEARNED FROM THEIR JOURNEYS 149
- APPLYING SUCCESS STRATEGIES 151

XXIII. THE FUTURE OF YOUTUBE 153
- EMERGING TRENDS IN CONTENT CREATION 154
- PREDICTIONS FOR THE PLATFORM 156
- ADAPTING TO FUTURE CHANGES 157

XXIV. COMMON MISTAKES TO AVOID 159
- PITFALLS IN CONTENT CREATION 160
- MISTAKES IN MARKETING STRATEGIES 162
- AVOIDING BURNOUT 163

XXV. RESOURCES FOR YOUTUBE CREATORS 165
- ONLINE COURSES AND TUTORIALS 166
- BOOKS AND GUIDES 167
- COMMUNITY SUPPORT GROUPS 169

XXVI. CONCLUSION 172
- RECAP OF KEY STRATEGIES 173
- ENCOURAGEMENT FOR ASPIRING CREATORS 174
- FINAL THOUGHTS ON YOUTUBE SUCCESS 176
- CALL TO ACTION FOR CONTINUED LEARNING 177

BIBLIOGRAPHY 179

I. INTRODUCTION

The rapid rise of YouTube as a platform for content creation and consumption has transformed how individuals communicate and share their stories. Emerging from humble beginnings, many YouTube creators embark on a journey characterized by creativity, perseverance, and strategic thinking. The allure of reaching millions of subscribers can be enticing, yet the path to get there is often fraught with challenges. This essay aims to demystify the process by breaking it down into actionable steps and strategies that have proven successful for numerous content creators. By examining the nuances of branding, audience engagement, and production quality, the discussion will highlight the essential components that contribute to sustained growth on the platform. Navigating the complexities of YouTube's algorithms and trends is key for aspiring content creators who wish to capture and retain audience attention. Understanding how the platforms algorithms prioritize certain content can greatly influence a creators ability to gain visibility. This essay will explore various tactics that enable creators to optimize their videos, ensuring they meet the criteria necessary for higher placement in search results and recommended feeds. The role of data analytics in shaping content strategies cannot be overlooked. By utilizing insights from viewership patterns and engagement metrics, creators can better tailor their offerings to align with audience preferences, fostering a deeper connection with viewers and ultimately, driving subscriber growth.

The journey to achieving millions of subscribers requires not only talent and creativity but also a keen understanding of marketing and social media dynamics. Consistency in content production is paramount, as it establishes a sense of reliability and anticipation among viewers. Adaptation is equally critical in today's fast-evolving digital landscape, where trends can shift overnight. This essay seeks to empower both beginners and seasoned creators by equipping them with innovative strategies that enhance their market presence. From leveraging social media to build brand awareness to understanding the intricacies of channel monetization, the insights provided will serve as a comprehensive guide for anyone looking to thrive on YouTube and make a lasting impact in the digital realm.

OVERVIEW OF YOUTUBE AS A PLATFORM

Launched in 2005, YouTube has evolved into a multifaceted platform that serves not only as a video-sharing site but also as a dynamic social network. This transformation allows content creators to engage with audiences worldwide, facilitating connections that go beyond the confines of traditional media. With over two billion monthly logged-in users, YouTube represents a significant opportunity for creators to tap into a broad and diverse demographic. The platform's intricate algorithms are designed to promote viewer retention, encouraging creators to focus on producing high-quality, engaging content that resonates with their audience. By understanding these algorithms and the ways in which they prioritize certain types of videos, creators can effectively enhance their visibility and attract more subscribers. Navigating YouTubes algorithmic landscape requires a strategic approach to content creation and marketing. Key elements include keyword optimization, effective video titles, and the use of engaging thumbnails to capture initial interest. Video metadata, such as descriptions and tags, plays a crucial role in ensuring that content is discoverable by the right audience. Creators must consider audience engagement metrics, such as watch time and likes, which significantly influence how frequently their videos are recommended. These factors highlight the importance of analytics in shaping content strategies and guiding creators toward producing videos that not only attract views but also foster a loyal subscriber base. By prioritizing these aspects, content producers can establish a strong presence on the platform and leverage their growth effectively.

Beyond its technical elements, YouTube also serves as a powerful platform for brand building and audience development. Successful creators often cultivate a personal brand that resonates with their viewers, allowing for authenticity and relatability to shine through their videos. This branding extends beyond content into social media marketing, where creators cultivate their online persona across various platforms, driving traffic back to their YouTube channels. Consistent content creation is paramount; regular uploads keep audiences engaged and eager for new material. Adaptability in response to evolving trends, viewer preferences, and platform updates is crucial for long-term success. By integrating these principles, aspiring YouTubers can not only grow their subscriber count but forge meaningful connections that cultivate community and loyalty among viewers.

IMPORTANCE OF SUBSCRIBER COUNT

A high subscriber count serves as a crucial indicator of a YouTube channels credibility and reach. In an era where digital consumption has risen dramatically, users often gravitate toward creators with larger followings, perceiving them as more trustworthy or entertaining. This consumer behavior is rooted in social proof; when viewers see that a channel has thousands or millions of subscribers, it inherently influences their perception and encourages them to join the fold. Consequently, a robust subscriber base not only amplifies views but also fosters a sense of community and belonging among viewers, reinforcing their engagement with the channels content. A substantial subscriber count opens the door to monetization opportunities, enabling creators to maximize their earnings through diversified revenue streams. Brands seeking influencers for partnerships often prioritize channels with significant followings to ensure their products reach a wide and engaged audience. This can lead to sponsorship deals, product placements, and affiliate marketing opportunities that can exponentially increase a creators income. YouTube itself rewards channels with a larger subscriber base by prioritizing their content in recommendations and search results, creating a virtuous cycle of visibility and revenue potential. The journey from zero to millions of subscribers encapsulates a creator's growth and adaptation to the ever-evolving landscape of the platform. This experience cultivates resilience, as content producers must continuously refine their skills, analyze audience feedback, and stay abreast of algorithm changes. The strategies that lead to subscriber growth—such as optimizing video titles and descriptions, utilizing effective thumbnail designs, and maintaining a consistent upload schedule—contribute to a creators overall mastery of the platform. Achieving a significant subscriber count not only symbolizes success but also represents a deep understanding of audience engagement and content optimization, essential elements for long-term sustainability in the competitive world of YouTube.

PURPOSE OF THE ESSAY

Amid the ever-evolving landscape of digital content, understanding the mechanisms behind YouTubes success can empower creators to carve out their niches. Achieving millions of subscribers requires a comprehensive grasp of content dynamics, audience engagement, and algorithm nuances. This essay endeavors to illuminate the various strategies that successful YouTubers implement, establishing a roadmap for novices and veterans alike. By dissecting techniques for brand building and authentic storytelling, readers will uncover the ingredients that allure viewers and keep them coming back for more. The synthesis of theory and practice will provide a well-rounded approach for aspiring creators eager to elevate their platforms.

Deciphering YouTube's algorithms plays a pivotal role in enhancing content visibility and reach. Many budding creators overlook the crucial relationship between video performance metrics and algorithmic promotion. In this essay, emphasis will be placed on analyzing key performance indicators such as watch time, click-through rate, and audience retention. Equipped with this knowledge, aspiring YouTubers can strategically tailor their content to align with algorithmic preferences, thereby broadening their audience and increasing subscriber counts. Techniques such as employing targeted keywords, engaging thumbnails, and optimal posting schedules will be explored to maximize potential viewership and subscriber growth. This exploration extends beyond mere technicalities; it also delves into the broader implications of community building and sustained engagement. The importance of establishing a loyal viewer base cannot be overstated in a social media environment dominated by fleeting attention spans. Creators must actively cultivate relationships with their audience, encouraging interaction and feedback through various channels. This essay aims to highlight the significance of consistency, adaptability, and innovative marketing strategies in fostering a thriving YouTube channel. By showcasing real-world examples of successful creators, the essay aims to motivate readers on their journey, equipping them with the tools necessary to not only start from zero but to thrive in an increasingly competitive arena.

II. UNDERSTANDING YOUTUBE

Navigating the complex landscape of YouTube demands an acute understanding of audience engagement and platform algorithms. Successful creators recognize that content must not only captivate but also resonate with specific viewer demographics. This involves crafting a distinct voice and narrative style that aligns with the interests and values of the target audience. By conducting thorough audience research, creators can identify trending topics and evergreen content that promise to attract and retain viewers. The importance of initial engagement, such as likes and comments, cannot be understated; these metrics fuel YouTubes recommendation system, prone to favor videos that spark interaction. In essence, understanding the audience—and what prompts them to engage—allows creators to produce content that fosters community, ultimately driving subscriber growth. Equally significant is the role of data analytics in shaping content strategy. YouTube provides a suite of tools that empower creators to dissect viewer behavior and performance metrics. Analyzing watch time, retention rates, and demographic information equips creators with insights that inform their content planning and delivery. Creators can determine which types of videos perform best and identify the moments when viewers drop off. Such insights facilitate not only targeted improvements to existing content but also inspire new video ideas that align with audience preferences. By understanding viewership patterns, creators can adapt their strategies to ensure longevity in a fast-evolving digital landscape, making data-driven decisions that foster growth and engagement. Adaptability has evolved into an essential trait for any YouTuber aiming for long-term success. The platform's algorithms and user preferences can shift dramatically, necessitating a flexible approach to content creation and marketing strategies. Creators must continuously learn and apply new skills, whether its embracing emerging trends like short-form videos or integrating live streaming into their repertoire. The ability to pivot based on feedback and data is crucial; what resonates with viewers today may not hold their attention tomorrow. By staying informed about industry trends and platform updates, creators position themselves to not only navigate challenges but also leverage opportunities for expansion. Thus, the journey through YouTube is not merely about producing content—it's a dynamic process of growth, learning, and resilience.

HISTORY AND EVOLUTION OF YOUTUBE

Launched in February 2005, the platform quickly transformed from a simple video-sharing site into a colossal multimedia icon. Early adopters included individuals and small entities who embraced the democratization of video content, uploading everything from personal vlogs to artistic short films. By November of that year, YouTube gained enough traction to catch the interest of Google, which acquired it in November 2006 for $1.65 billion in stock. This acquisition catalyzed substantial changes, including the introduction of better infrastructure, enhanced user experience, and monetization opportunities for creators. The company's growing commitment to improving content quality and accessibility, coupled with robust advertising capabilities, positioned YouTube as an essential platform for marketing and entertainment. As digital landscapes evolved, YouTube kept pace with these transformations. The introduction of features such as live streaming, 360-degree video, and Super Chat expanded creative possibilities for content creators. The partnership program launched in 2007 allowed creators to earn revenue through ads, fostering a vibrant ecosystem that incentivized high-quality content production. Strategic changes implemented in algorithms altered visibility, pushing creators to understand their audience better and focus on engagement. YouTube also began emphasizing community building, as seen through features like subscriptions, comments, and community posts. These innovations helped nurture a dynamic space where creators could foster loyal viewer relationships, ultimately expanding their reach and influence. With the emergence of mobile-first consumption habits and the rise of social media platforms, YouTube has further adapted its strategy to maintain relevance. The launch of YouTube Shorts in 2020 positioned the platform as a competitor within the burgeoning vertical video market. This strategic pivot tapped into the growing preference for bite-sized content akin to that found on TikTok. YouTubes algorithm continues to evolve, becoming increasingly sophisticated in promoting videos that enhance viewer engagement. These shifts present challenges for content creators who must remain agile in their approaches while also capitalizing on emerging trends. By embracing change and learning to leverage new features, creators can navigate this interconnected digital ecosystem, thereby reinforcing their foothold in the competitive landscape that YouTube has cultivated over nearly two decades.

YOUTUBE'S ROLE IN DIGITAL MEDIA
An exploration of YouTube reveals its transformation from a mere video-sharing platform to a cornerstone of digital media,

impacting both creators and audiences alike. This evolution is underscored by its pioneering role in democratizing content creation, allowing anyone with internet access to share their voice. Consequently, traditional media outlets have had to adapt their strategies to engage viewers who increasingly prefer the authenticity and relatability that YouTube offers. As millions of content creators upload videos daily, the platform cultivates a diverse array of perspectives and narratives, enriching the overall media landscape. This shift not only challenges established norms but also encourages innovative storytelling techniques as creators experiment with formats, genres, and styles in pursuit of audience engagement. In addition to shaping content creation, YouTubes algorithms play a pivotal role in defining what content becomes popular. The recommendation system serves to connect viewers with topics that align with their interests, drastically influencing viewing habits and trends. Through data-driven insights, content creators can optimize their videos to align with trending keywords, viewer preferences, and engagement metrics. In this context, understanding algorithmic intricacies allows creators to enhance their visibility and reach, creating a symbiotic relationship between the platform's technology and user-generated content. The interplay of community dynamics and algorithmic precision fosters an environment where success is achievable but requires strategic thinking, consistent effort, and a commitment to understanding audience behaviors. YouTube has revolutionized monetization strategies within the digital media sphere, allowing creators to turn passion into profit. As the platform introduces features like Super Chats, channel memberships, and ad revenue sharing, it empowers content creators to generate sustainable income from their channels. This diversification of revenue streams not only incentivizes adherence to YouTubes community guidelines but also encourages creators to innovate their content continuously. Successful creators leverage platforms outside of YouTube, intertwining social media marketing with their channel growth strategies to broaden their reach and engagement. This multifaceted approach to monetization illustrates how YouTube not only shapes the landscape of digital media but also redefines the creator economy, making the path to success both complex and accessible for aspiring influencers.

DEMOGRAPHICS OF YOUTUBE USERS

Content creators must understand the diverse landscape of YouTubes user demographics to tailor their strategies effectively. The platform attracts a wide range of viewers, reflecting a dynamic global audience with varying interests and preferences. According to a 2023 Pew Research Center study, approximately 81% of U.S. adults aged 18 to 29 utilize YouTube, underscoring its dominance among younger demographics. In contrast, about 50% of those aged 65 and older also engage with the platform. These statistics reveal that while youth remains at the forefront of YouTubes viewer base, older age groups are increasingly drawn to its vast array of content, thus expanding potential market segments for creators. Understanding these demographics helps in crafting messages and content types that resonate well with targeted audiences.

The gender composition of YouTube users offers significant insights for creators seeking to refine their content strategies. Research indicates that while the platform has a near-even split between male and female users, there are noteworthy variances in content consumption patterns. Women are more likely to engage with lifestyle, beauty, and wellness content, whereas men predominantly gravitate toward gaming, technology, and sports. Such distinctions emphasize the importance of aligning content creation with the preferences of specific demographic segments. Creators should consider the unique interests of subgroups within these categories, as niche audiences can often lead to heightened engagement and loyalty. By identifying and targeting the dominant demographics, creators can craft content that is not only appealing but also fosters a deeper connection with their viewer base.

The geographical diversity of YouTubes audience presents both challenges and opportunities for creators aiming for millions of subscribers. The platform caters to a global audience, with significant viewership concentrated in the United States, India, Brazil, and Indonesia, among others. This geographic variation influences content themes, language, and cultural references. Creators must be adept at recognizing these differences and adapting their messages accordingly. A creator appealing primarily to a U.S. audience may need to localize their content to resonate with viewers from other regions, which could include incorporating multilingual captions or culturally relevant examples. By embracing the rich tapestry of YouTubes user demographics, creators can enhance their reach and engagement, setting the foundation for sustained growth and success on the platform.

III. CREATING A YOUTUBE CHANNEL

Establishing a unique channel identity is pivotal for attracting and retaining subscribers within the competitive landscape of YouTube. Content creators must begin by defining their niche, which not only highlights their passions and expertise but also fills a gap in the existing market. This involves conducting thorough research to understand audience preferences, trending topics, and the strengths of potential competitors. A compelling channel identity includes a consistent visual theme, such as logos and banner designs, as well as a distinct tone or voice that reflects the creator's personality. It is crucial to develop a captivating channel description that effectively conveys the value the channel offers. Engaging intros, consistent video formats, and recognizable outros create a sense of familiarity that audiences come to expect, which fosters loyalty and encourages subscriptions. By establishing a strong brand identity, creators lay the groundwork for a sustainable and engaging community. Consistency in content creation serves as the bedrock upon which successful YouTube channels are built. Regular uploads not only keep existing subscribers engaged but also optimize the channel for the algorithms that govern video visibility. Creators should develop a content calendar that outlines their posting schedule while balancing spontaneity and strategic planning to respond to audience feedback and emerging trends. This practice also includes maintaining a standard video quality, which encompasses technical aspects such as sound and lighting, as well as narrative cohesion and visual appeal. By delivering high-quality content consistently, creators increase the likelihood of viewer retention and growth. This dedication to an upload timetable signals professionalism and commitment, enhancing trust among potential subscribers. As creators build a loyal following, their audience begins to anticipate new content, thereby expanding their reach through heightened engagement and word-of-mouth promotion.

Utilizing analytics tools effectively allows creators to fine-tune their strategies and maximize growth potential. YouTube provides a wealth of data about viewer behavior, watch time, and demographics, which can inform decisions regarding content direction, posting times, and audience engagement tactics. Analyzing this data helps creators identify which videos resonate most with their viewers, allowing them to replicate successful elements in future content. Tracking subscriber growth and engagement trends grants valuable insight into the effectiveness of promotional efforts across social media and other platforms. Embracing a feedback-loop approach by regularly refining content based on analytics ensures that creators remain adaptable to changing viewer preferences and platform dynamics. Through diligent use of data insights, creators not only enhance the quality of their output but also bolster the sustainable growth of their channels, bringing them one step closer to reaching millions of subscribers.

CHOOSING A NICHE

Identifying a niche is a fundamental step that can significantly impact a creators journey on YouTube. By honing in on a specific area of interest, content producers can ensure that their videos attract a dedicated audience, increasing viewer retention and ultimately fostering community engagement. A well-defined niche allows creators to differentiate themselves from the vast array of content available on the platform, making it easier for potential subscribers to recognize what sets them apart. Niche content often garners a more passionate following, as it resonates deeply with viewers who share specific interests or needs. This targeted approach not only assists in establishing a strong brand identity but also enhances the potential for collaboration with other influencers within the same space, multiplying growth opportunities. Once a niche has been identified, understanding the audience is critical for sustaining long-term engagement. Conducting thorough research on viewer preferences, habits, and demographics can provide invaluable insights into what types of content will resonate most. Utilizing tools such as Google Trends or YouTube Analytics can help gauge which topics within a chosen niche are currently gaining traction. Creators must remain adaptable; audience interests can evolve, and being aware of these shifts allows for timely content adjustments. Engaging with the community through comments and social media platforms can further strengthen this connection, enabling creators to tailor their content to meet evolving viewer expectations. Creating a feedback loop not only encourages loyalty but also cultivates an environment where subscribers feel valued and heard. The process of choosing and developing a niche requires strategic foresight and continuous effort. Success on YouTube is rarely instantaneous; it demands patience, persistence, and a willingness to experiment. As creators delve deeper into their specialized area, they may find opportunities for innovation within established content conventions. By consistently producing quality videos that align with their niche while exploring diverse formats and themes, creators can keep their content fresh and engaging. This not only solidifies their position within the niche but also positions them for potential growth beyond it. As the YouTube landscape continues to evolve, maintaining a balance between niche specificity and broader relevance will empower creators to adapt and thrive, ultimately paving the way for a successful and sustainable YouTube career.

SETTING UP YOUR CHANNEL

Creating an effective channel begins with a strong foundation, where clarity of purpose plays a crucial role. Content creators must first define their niche, as this not only positions them within a specific community but also helps attract a targeted audience. By researching existing content, a creator can identify gaps in the market, which allows them to present unique offerings. Choosing a channel name that reflects this niche is equally important; it should be memorable and easily associated with the content. A compelling channel description, incorporating relevant keywords, sets the stage for viewers and enhances discoverability. In this initial phase, laying out a cohesive vision not only informs future content but also aids in establishing a consistent brand across the platform, ultimately positioning the channel for growth and longevity.

Once the foundational elements are in place, the next step focuses on visual aesthetics and branding. An attractive channel banner and logo are essential components that contribute to the overall perception of professionalism. This singular visual identity creates an inviting atmosphere, encouraging potential subscribers to click and explore further. The creator should craft an engaging trailer that encapsulates what viewers can expect from the channel, establishing a robust first impression. Consistency in video thumbnails and formatting plays a significant role as well; recognizable styles will help viewers identify the channels content amidst the vast sea of videos on YouTube. This cohesive branding acts as a powerful tool for differentiation and retention, ensuring that once viewers land on the channel, they are more likely to subscribe and remain engaged over time.

The technical aspects of setting up the channel should not be overlooked, as they play a vital role in the creators overall success. Configuring video settings—such as optimizing titles, descriptions, and tags—enhances the chances of appearing in search results. Familiarity with YouTubes algorithm can greatly influence a channels reach; algorithms prioritize engagement, so understanding how to encourage likes, shares, and comments is crucial. Creators should explore the monetization options available through the platform, which can impact content strategy moving forward. Establishing clear analytics helps creators track performance and adjust their methods accordingly. By remaining adaptable and responsive to the data collected, creators maximize their potential for growth and sustainability in the dynamic world of YouTube, paving the way for long-term success and an ever-expanding subscriber base.

CRAFTING A CHANNEL DESCRIPTION

A compelling channel description serves as the anchor that attracts viewers and communicates the essence of your content at a glance. In a landscape flooded with options, your description must encapsulate what makes your channel unique, whether that be your distinctive voice, specialized niche, or innovative approach to storytelling. The initial lines should strike a chord with viewers by highlighting the value they will gain from subscribing, using engaging language that reflects your personality. Rather than merely listing content types, infusing enthusiasm and purpose into your description can captivate potential subscribers and encourage them to explore further. Clearly stating your goals—for instance, building a community or sharing expertise—can foster a connection between you and your audience, making your channel feel more inviting and relatable.

Employing strategic keywords throughout the channel description is essential for discoverability. YouTube operates as a search engine, meaning that keyword optimization plays a crucial role in how potential subscribers find your content. Identifying relevant terms that resonate with your target audience can significantly improve your visibility in search results. Balancing these keywords within a narrative structure can prevent your description from feeling like a bland sales pitch; it is about weaving them into the narrative of your channel. This not only aids in search optimization but also enriches the overall storytelling aspect of your channel, making it more appealing to a broader audience. Regularly revisiting and adjusting these keywords based on trends or shifts in audience interest can help keep your channel dynamic and relevant.

Maintaining an authentic voice and consistent branding throughout the description not only reinforces your channel's identity but also enhances viewer trust and loyalty. Your description should mirror the tone of your videos and include visual elements or emojis that align with your brand, creating a coherent experience for viewers across platforms. Including a call-to-action encourages potential subscribers to take a step further, whether it is prompting them to hit the subscribe button, engage in comments, or connect with you on other social media. As your channel evolves, revisiting and refining your description is essential; updates can reflect changes in content style, audience engagement, or personal growth as a creator. An effective channel description is a living element of your branding strategy, dynamically supporting your journey toward securing a dedicated viewer base and achieving your goals on YouTube.

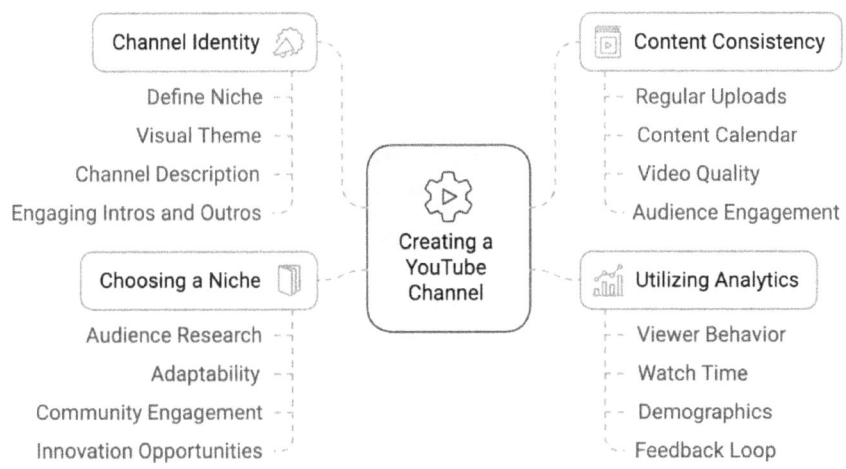

IV. DEVELOPING A CONTENT STRATEGY

A comprehensive content strategy is foundational to capturing and retaining audience interest on YouTube. Initially, it involves conducting thorough market research to identify target demographics, preferences, and trending topics within the niche. By analyzing competitors, creators can discern what content resonates with viewers while also identifying gaps that their own videos can fill. This research phase provides critical insights into audience behavior, leading to the development of a unique value proposition. The aim is to craft content that not only entertains or informs but also stands out amidst the multitude of competing channels. By setting specific objectives—be it subscriber growth or enhanced viewer engagement—creators can create a roadmap that guides their content development process. Following the research, the next phase of a content strategy emphasizes the importance of planning and consistency. It involves creating a content calendar that outlines when and what type of videos will be released. This structured approach not only helps maintain regular uploads, which is crucial for audience retention, but also allows creators to strategically align their output with significant dates or events in their niche. Leveraging various content formats—such as tutorials, vlogs, and interviews—can cater to diverse viewer preferences, maximizing engagement opportunities. Adaptability in content planning is vital; creators should stay alert to analytical data and audience feedback, allowing them to pivot or refine their approach in real-time while retaining the core themes that define their channel. Measuring the success of a content strategy hinges on utilizing YouTube's analytic tools to track performance metrics. Key indicators such as watch time, click-through rates, and engagement levels provide actionable insights into what content thrives and what may fall flat. Creators should assess these metrics regularly to determine the effectiveness of their strategy, enabling them to make informed adjustments that enhance viewer satisfaction and retention. Fostering a community by actively engaging with viewers through comments or social media can generate loyalty that is invaluable for subscriber growth. A well-executed content strategy not only drives a channel's immediate success but also builds a sustainable brand that can evolve with audience demands and platform changes over time.

IDENTIFYING TARGET AUDIENCE

Understanding the preferences and behaviors of viewers is essential for any YouTube creator aiming to build a substantial following. Engaging with a target audience begins with thorough research that uncovers their interests, demographics, and viewing habits. Tools such as Google Trends, YouTube Analytics, and audience surveys can provide valuable insights into what specific groups seek in video content. A content creator focused on cooking tutorials, for instance, must identify whether their potential audience prefers quick meal prep ideas, vegan recipes, or gourmet cooking techniques. This strategic approach not only aids in content creation but also positions the creator as a relevant voice in the community, ultimately fostering loyalty and engagement. Another vital aspect of identifying a target audience is the iterative nature of content development. As creators produce videos and interact with viewers, they must remain vigilant, analyzing feedback and evolving trends that can inform their approach. If a particular style of video garners greater engagement, it might signal a shift in viewer preference that the creator can capitalize on. Being receptive to audience feedback, whether through comments or direct messages, allows creators to create a dynamic relationship with their viewers, fostering an environment where subscribers feel valued and invested in the creators journey. This adaptive strategy not only enhances content relevance but also helps establish a more engaged community around the channel. Recognizing the target audiences needs extends beyond initial research and feedback; it requires ongoing commitment to fostering authentic community interactions. Creators can enhance viewer loyalty by building a brand persona that resonates with their audience. This connection can be achieved through consistent communication, personal anecdotes, or even addressing viewers by name in comments and videos. Such practices go a long way in creating a sense of belonging among viewers, which, in turn, can stimulate word-of-mouth marketing and organic channel growth. By solidifying this bond, creators not only amplify their reach but also lay a strong foundation for long-term success on the platform, transforming casual viewers into dedicated subscribers.

CONTENT TYPES AND FORMATS

The diversity of content types is one of the defining features of YouTube, allowing creators to engage with audiences in various ways. Vlogs, for instance, provide an intimate glimpse into a creators daily life, fostering a connection that can translate into loyalty and higher engagement rates. On the other hand, instructional videos or tutorials offer viewers valuable knowledge, enticing them to return for future learning experiences. The incorporation of challenges or skits injects entertainment and spontaneity into a channel, appealing to a broader demographic. As creators experiment with these formats, they often discover unique ways to amalgamate them, such as blending a tutorial with a personal narrative, thereby enriching the viewing experience. Understanding and utilizing these diverse content genres becomes crucial for creators aiming to establish a strong presence within the competitive landscape of YouTube.

Each content format not only varies in style but also in its potential for audience engagement and monetization. Live streams, for example, foster real-time interaction between creators and their viewers, creating a sense of community and urgency that can significantly boost subscriber loyalty. Meanwhile, pre-recorded content offers opportunities for editing and refinement, allowing creators to present their best selves to the audience. Short-form content, such as YouTube Shorts, has surged in popularity, enabling creators to convey messages quickly and effectively, which is particularly appealing in an age of dwindling attention spans. Analytics play a critical role in determining which formats resonate most with a target audience; hence, creators should leverage data to refine their strategies. By comparing metrics across various types of content, creators can identify trends and preferences, optimizing their future productions to meet viewer expectations and bolster channel growth.

The strategic implementation of these diverse content formats requires a keen understanding of audience demographics and engagement behaviors. Creators must be attuned to the preferences of their target viewers, ensuring that their content aligns with both audience interests and overarching trends. Incorporating elements like trending challenges or socially relevant themes can enhance relevance and foster broader discussion within the community. Consistency in both posting schedules and content themes is vital; it not only strengthens brand identity but also keeps audiences returning for more. As algorithms prioritize viewer retention and engagement, successful creators must adeptly navigate these elements, adapting their strategies in response to evolving viewer behaviors and platform updates. Consequently, those who are flexible and innovative in their approach to content types and formats stand the greatest chance of achieving sustained growth and subscriber retention on YouTube.

PLANNING A CONTENT CALENDAR

Establishing a consistent release schedule is pivotal in engaging a YouTube audience effectively. Content calendars serve as strategic tools that enable creators to map out their video ideas, align them with audience preferences, and maintain a regular upload routine. By establishing specific days for content release, channels can foster viewer anticipation and build a loyal subscriber base. Without such planning, creators often risk falling into the trap of sporadic uploads, which can diminish audience engagement and affect overall channel growth. A structured schedule allows for the timely incorporation of seasonal topics or trending themes, optimizing the relevance of content. Engaging with viewers via comments or social media should also inform how content is shaped and when it gets published, allowing for a more responsive and adaptive approach.

In addition to scheduling, thoughtful content categorization is crucial for maximizing audience interest. When devising a content calendar, creators should consider diverse themes or formats that will appeal to their target demographic. This could include tutorials, vlogs, challenges, or interviews, all of which can attract varied viewer groups, thereby increasing overall channel reach. To maintain a balanced and engaging calendar, it is also beneficial to rotate these categories on a regular basis, ensuring that the content feels fresh and appealing. Collaborating with other creators can diversify the content portfolio and tap into new audience segments, thus expanding visibility. By creating a well-rounded calendar that reflects both the creators strengths and audience interests, growth opportunities multiply, reinforcing the significance of strategic planning in driving subscriber growth. Reviewing and adapting the content calendar should be an ongoing process informed by analytics and viewer feedback. Utilizing YouTubes analytical tools allows creators to assess which videos perform well, how audiences interact, and what resonates most strongly with viewers. By identifying patterns and preferences, adjustments to the content calendar can be made, ensuring relevance over time. This iterative process not only enhances content quality but also builds a dynamic relationship with subscribers who feel their opinions and interests are valued. A flexible yet structured approach to content planning leads to sustained growth, transforming initial subscriber spikes into enduring engagement. In a rapidly evolving digital landscape, remaining responsive to audience needs sets successful channels apart, illustrating the critical role of a meticulous content calendar in the journey from obscurity to prominence on YouTube.

Content Type	Key Features	Engagement Benefits	Audience Growth
Tutorials	Educational format, step-by-step guides.	High educational value, ideal for niche audiences.	Recurrent subscriptions for more specialized content.
Vlogs	Personal, daily life content.	Strong emotional connection, creator closeness.	Organic growth through loyal followers.
Interviews	Conversations with experts.	Unique insights, new perspectives.	Attracts new audiences, growth via collaborations.
Unboxings/Reviews	Product presentations, opinions.	Sparks conversation, engages niche communities.	Attracts product-focused audience, good retention.
Challenges/Trends	Trend-based, viral content.	Immediate engagement, direct participation.	Rapid growth through viral content.
Documentaries	In-depth, well-produced narratives.	High engagement from meaningful content.	Strong retention in niche areas with complex topics.
Live Streaming	Real-time interaction.	Strong direct engagement, active community.	Growth through constant interaction, fosters loyalty.

V. BUILDING A PERSONAL BRAND

Crafting an authentic identity is paramount in the world of YouTube, where countless creators compete for the attention of viewers. A well-defined personal brand resonates with audiences, establishing a sense of trust and relatability that enhances viewer loyalty. This requires a clear understanding of one's values, skills, and unique perspectives, which inform the content produced. A creator's narrative should weave together their background, motivations, and aspirations, creating a storyline that not only entertains but also engages viewers on a deeper level. By consistently aligning their content with this narrative, creators ensure that their personal brand becomes memorable and distinctive, setting them apart in a saturated market. Equally important is the visual and thematic consistency that a personal brand should embody across all platforms. From logo designs to color schemes and video thumbnails, maintaining a cohesive aesthetic reinforces brand recognition and professionalism. This visual language should reflect the creators personality and the type of content they produce, whether it is educational, entertaining, or inspirational. Engagement strategies, such as interactive polls and open-ended questions in videos, further enhance this connection by inviting viewer participation. By thoughtfully curating all elements that contribute to their online persona, creators not only attract subscribers but also foster a community that feels invested in their journey.

Building a personal brand requires ongoing reflection and adaptability, as trends and audience preferences can shift rapidly. Monitoring audience feedback and analytics is essential for creators to understand what resonates most with their viewers.

By evaluating which types of content garner the most engagement, creators can adjust their strategies to remain relevant and appealing. Staying informed about changes in YouTube's policies and algorithms allows creators to pivot their branding approach as needed. A dynamic personal brand not only helps to attract new subscribers but also sustains long-term engagement, positioning creators for continued growth and success amidst the evolving landscape of digital content creation.

CREATING A UNIQUE IDENTITY

A distinctive online identity acts as the foundation for any successful YouTube channel. Establishing this identity involves articulating a clear vision that resonates with the creators passion and values while appealing to a target audience. Content creators should reflect on their unique skills and experiences, as these elements set them apart in an oversaturated market. A creator passionate about sustainable living might focus on eco-friendly lifestyle choices, blending personal anecdotes with informative content. This approach fosters a sense of authenticity, allowing viewers to connect on a personal level. Developing a unique identity not only defines the creator's brand but also serves to attract a loyal audience that shares similar interests, creating an engaged community around the channel.

To enhance this unique identity, visual branding and storytelling play critical roles in creating a cohesive aesthetic and narrative. This means not only employing consistent color schemes and logos but also curating a style that reflects the creators personality. Effective storytelling captures the audience's attention, ensuring that viewers remain engaged throughout the video. Integrating personal experiences or relatable situations can deepen emotional connections with audiences, making each video memorable. Creators should leverage platform features, such as end screens and thumbnails, to present a visually appealing narrative that invites exploration of further content. By ensuring that each visual element aligns with the established identity, creators can solidify their brand, encouraging subscribers to return for more and fostering a sense of belonging within their community. Regular reflection and adjustment are vital to sustaining a unique identity as trends and audience preferences evolve. Creators must analyze engagement metrics and feedback to ensure their content continues to resonate with viewers, adapting their approach without compromising their core values. This may involve experimenting with various formats, topics, or even collaboration with other creators to introduce fresh perspectives. Understanding the balance between established identity and innovation is crucial; maintaining a fixed image can lead to stagnation, while too much experimentation can alienate loyal viewers. Striking this balance allows creators to not only retain their unique identity but also grow alongside their audience, continually enriching the channels content and ensuring long-term success. By making these adjustments, creators can effectively navigate the dynamic landscape of YouTube, evolving their brand while remaining true to their original vision.

DESIGNING CHANNEL ART AND LOGO

Creating a visually appealing and cohesive brand identity is paramount for any aspiring YouTube creator. The first impression of a channel often comes from its channel art and logo, which serve as visual anchors for potential subscribers. Effective channel art not only conveys the essence of the content but also reflects the creators unique personality and style. To achieve a professional appearance, it's essential to utilize high-quality graphics, consistent color schemes, and readable fonts. These elements should collectively narrate a story that resonates with the target audience, fostering an immediate emotional connection that invites viewers to explore further. Elements such as thumbnails must align with the overarching channel theme, ensuring a uniform aesthetic that enhances the brand's visibility across the platform. Equally important is the logo, a compact emblem that encapsulates the channels identity in a memorable way. A well-designed logo operates on multiple levels; it should be recognizable, versatile, and simple enough to look good across various mediums, whether it's on a smartphone, a website banner, or promotional materials. In crafting a logo, creators should consider their unique selling proposition—what makes them stand out from the vast array of competitors on YouTube. Engaging with graphic design tools or hiring a professional designer can ensure that the final product resonates with the intended audience and elevates the overall brand perception. This visual identity not only establishes credibility but also lays the groundwork for long-term audience loyalty, as subscribers are more likely to return to a channel with a polished and consistent visual aesthetic. In the ever-evolving landscape of YouTube, the significance of channel art and logos extends beyond mere aesthetics; they are integral elements of a strategic branding approach. As creators navigate their path from obscurity to prominence, leveraging these design components effectively can enhance discoverability and memorability, establishing a strong foothold in a competitive market. Crafting channel art and logos that communicate professionalism and authenticity reinforces the creators commitment to quality, further engaging viewers. As content evolves, so too should the branding; creators must remain adaptable, updating their visual elements to reflect new directions or shifts in audience preferences. Investing thought and creativity into channel art and logos can catalyze a channels growth, transforming casual viewers into dedicated subscribers, thus playing a pivotal role in achieving the milestone of millions of followers.

ESTABLISHING A CONSISTENT VOICE

Crafting a distinctive voice is essential for creators seeking to connect authentically with their audience. This voice encapsulates the personality, tone, and style that resonate throughout the content, allowing viewers to make a personal connection with the creator. Establishing a consistent voice requires careful consideration of the target audiences preferences and expectations. A creator who delivers content in a manner that aligns with their inherent persona fosters authenticity, making it easier for viewers to engage and invest emotionally. This voice needs to permeate every aspect of production—from the scripting and editing choices to the video thumbnails or social media interactions—ensuring that all elements are harmonized and recognizable. Successful creators often differentiate themselves by infusing humor, empathy, or expertise into their narratives, effectively cementing their status in the minds of viewers while simultaneously influencing subscriber growth.

Developing consistency in voice does not imply stagnancy; rather, it allows for organic evolution over time. Changes in trends, technology, or personal experiences can influence the creator's voice, which needs to be adapted thoughtfully to maintain viewer loyalty. Regularly revisiting and refining voice allows content creators to stay relevant while avoiding alienation of long-time followers. A creator may initially adopt a highly scripted format to convey research-driven content, but over time, they might evolve towards a more spontaneous conversational style as they grow more comfortable on camera and become increasingly attuned to their audiences desires. This evolution should be gradual and well-articulated; sudden shifts can disrupt audience trust and diminish months or years of brand development. Maintaining engagement through this adaptive strategy keeps the content dynamic, ensuring that it continues to resonate with both new and existing subscribers.

A consistent voice serves as the backbone of a creators brand identity, providing a solid foundation for engagement and growth. By maintaining this element, creators foster community and a sense of belonging among their audience, which is critical for long-term success. Engaging with followers through comments or social media platforms enhances this relationship, allowing for a two-way dialogue that can further refine the voice and content strategy. Creators who invite feedback and genuinely respond to their audience cultivate a sense of inclusion, making viewers feel valued and heard. This participatory approach not only strengthens the creators voice but also enhances viewer loyalty, encouraging organic growth through word-of-mouth recommendations. In summary, establishing and maintaining a consistent voice is integral to a creators journey on YouTube, directly impacting their ability to attract and retain an engaged audience.

VI. VIDEO PRODUCTION BASICS

Creating compelling video content begins with understanding the essential elements of production, which include pre-production, production, and post-production phases. During pre-production, its crucial to brainstorm ideas, develop a script, and create a storyboard that outlines the visual flow of the video. This planning ensures that the creator has a clear vision and purpose, which greatly enhances the quality of the final product. Logistical aspects like location scouting, scheduling, and securing equipment must be addressed to streamline the shooting process. A well-prepared pre-production phase minimizes potential setbacks during filming and can lead to a more polished end result. Once the groundwork is set, the production phase immerses the creator in actual filming, where proper techniques can significantly impact the videos effectiveness. Lighting, sound, and camera angles must be meticulously managed to create visually appealing and engaging content. Utilizing multiple cameras and microphones can enhance the production quality, allowing for dynamic shots and clear audio. Being adaptable during this phase is vital, as unexpected challenges may arise. Filmmakers should be mechanically adept and creatively flexible, ensuring that even unplanned moments can contribute positively to the overall narrative and engage viewers.

The journey does not end with filming; post-production is where the project truly comes to life. Editing is key to refining the content, involving the selection of the best footage, sound design, and the addition of visuals or music that align with the intended tone. This stage is also crucial for ensuring the final video is cohesive, engaging, and optimized for YouTubes user experience. Effective transitions, appropriate pacing, and thoughtful inclusion of graphics can elevate a video from mundane to exceptional. Understanding the importance of metadata—like titles, descriptions, and tags—can significantly boost visibility on the platform. By mastering these production basics, creators lay a solid foundation for building a successful YouTube channel that resonates with audiences and drives subscriber growth.

EQUIPMENT AND SOFTWARE NEEDS

Creating compelling content on YouTube necessitates not just creativity and strategic thinking but also a well-rounded arsenal of equipment and software. High-quality audio and video are crucial for attracting and retaining subscribers. Investing in a reliable camera, such as a DSLR or mirrorless camera, allows for superior image quality that can significantly enhance the viewing experience. Good lighting equipment, such as softbox lights or ring lights, can dramatically improve video clarity and visual appeal. For audio, using an external microphone is essential to capture crisp sound, as poor audio can deter viewers more than poor video quality. These foundational elements lay the groundwork for content that genuinely engages an audience and stands out in a crowded platform.

In parallel with physical equipment, the choice of software greatly impacts the production quality and efficiency of video creation. Video editing software, like Adobe Premiere Pro or Final Cut Pro, offers extensive features that enable creators to refine their content, add graphics, and produce polished final products. Tools like Canva for graphic design and Audacity for audio editing can elevate the professionalism of the content.

Social media management tools, such as Hootsuite or Buffer, help in scheduling posts and tracking engagement across platforms. Leveraging these software tools not only streamlines the production process but also allows creators to allocate more time to content ideation and audience engagement, both of which are critical for growth on the platform.

The effective use of analytics software can transform a creators approach to content strategy and user engagement. Platforms like YouTube Analytics and Google Trends provide invaluable insights into viewer behavior, demographics, and preferences. Understanding these analytics allows creators to tailor their content to better suit their audiences interests, which can lead to increased visibility and subscriber growth. Staying abreast of industry-standard SEO tools, such as TubeBuddy or VidIQ, can further aid in optimizing titles, tags, and descriptions for greater discoverability. By strategically integrating these equipment and software solutions, creators establish a solid foundation that not only enhances content creation but also fosters significant audience growth and engagement in their YouTube journey.

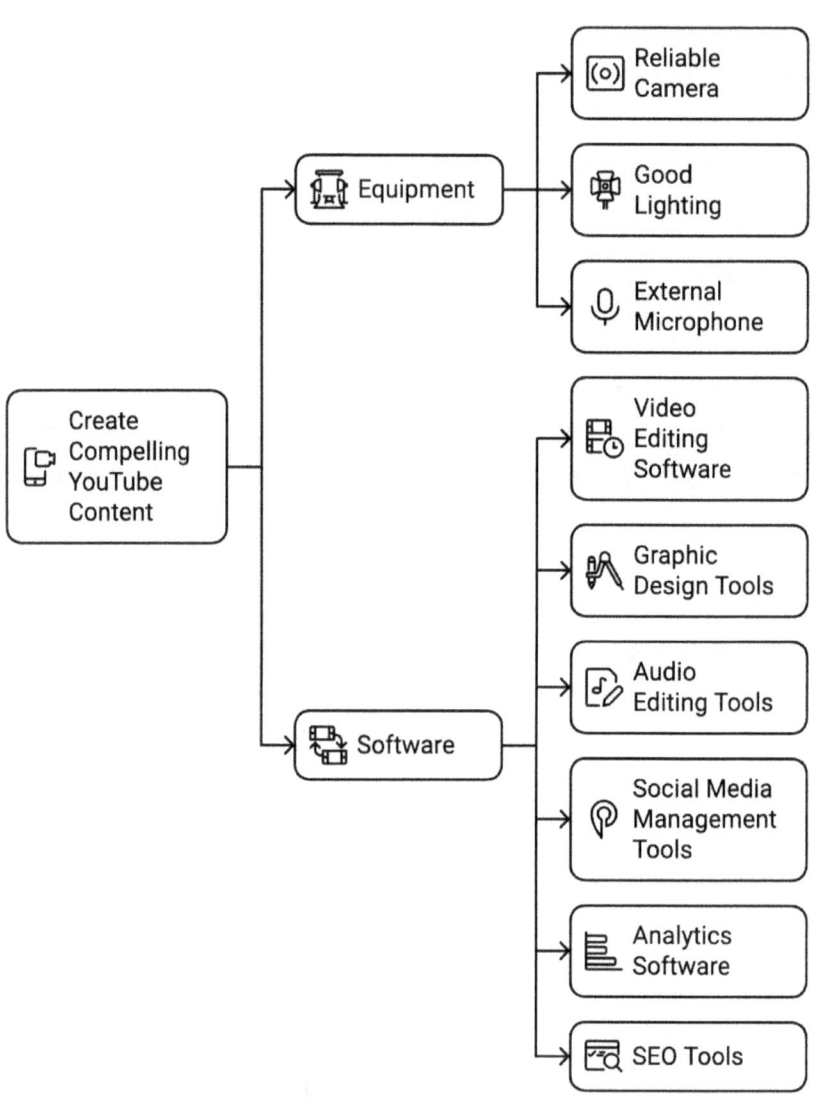

SCRIPTING AND STORYBOARDING

Effective content production hinges on meticulous planning, emphasizing the importance of scripting and storyboarding. By meticulously scripting videos, creators can articulate their messages clearly and persuasively, ensuring that every word serves a purpose. A well-crafted script acts as a roadmap, providing a structured narrative that guides both the creator and the viewer through the intended experience. This foundation allows for the equitable distribution of time and focus, shedding light on pivotal moments that engage audiences. Scripting helps streamline the editing process, reducing the amount of extraneous footage and minimizing the potential for post-production headaches, which is especially crucial for creators who aim to upload consistently. Complementing the scripting process, storyboarding transforms abstract concepts into tangible visuals, allowing creators to visualize the flow of their videos. Each frame serves as a storyboard cell, capturing key actions and emotions in a way that transcends mere textual descriptions. This visual planning not only enhances the clarity of ideas but also facilitates collaboration among team members, ensuring everyone is aligned on the projects vision. A thoughtfully constructed storyboard encourages consideration of camera angles, lighting, and overall aesthetic, thereby elevating the production quality. For YouTube creators, where first impressions can make or break a channel, effective storyboarding enhances the likelihood of captivating content that retains viewer attention from start to finish.

The integration of scripting and storyboarding contributes significantly to a creator's ability to grow a loyal subscriber base. These foundational steps allow for the creation of polished, coherent videos that resonate with audiences on a deeper level.

By delivering content that feels intentional and engaging, creators can cultivate a strong sense of connection and trust with their viewers, which is paramount in the crowded YouTube landscape. This preparatory work lays the groundwork for maximizing the impact of each video, opening doors to greater opportunities for engagement, shares, and ultimately, subscriber growth. By mastering these fundamental techniques, aspiring YouTubers not only enhance their storytelling abilities but also position themselves for long-term success in the platforms competitive ecosystem.

FILMING TECHNIQUES

Innovative filming techniques are pivotal in capturing the attention of YouTube audiences and elevating content quality. A crucial element is the use of varied camera angles, which can dramatically affect how a story is perceived. Choosing a close-up shot during an emotional moment establishes intimacy, while wide shots can provide context and showcase the environment, enriching the narrative. Employing techniques such as tracking shots or creative transitions can enhance the visual storytelling, making scenes more dynamic and engaging. Understanding lighting plays a significant role in setting the mood; soft, diffused lighting can evoke a romantic feeling, while harsher lighting can create tension or drama. These techniques not only serve to beautify the frame but also to deepen viewer connection and earnestness within the content, crucial aspects that can differentiate a creators work in the increasingly saturated YouTube marketplace. Sound design, often overlooked in favor of visual elements, profoundly influences audience retention and emotional response. The integration of high-quality audio can elevate a video from unremarkable to compelling. Utilizing background music that complements the tone of the narrative can subtly enhance viewer engagement, while sound effects often make scenes come alive; a well-timed sound cue can elicit laughter or draw gasps from an audience. Clear, professional-quality dialogue recording is imperative—poor sound can lead to viewer disengagement, regardless of how visually stunning a video may be. Filmmakers can employ techniques such as voice-over narration to guide viewers through complex narratives or to add an additional layer of commentary.

By masterfully pairing sound with visuals, content creators harness a powerful tool that enriches storytelling, creating a more immersive experience for subscribers and fostering loyalty within their audience.

Editing serves as the backbone of successful content creation on YouTube. A well-executed edit can improve pacing, enhance storytelling, and maintain viewer interest. Implementing techniques such as jump cuts can streamline narratives, removing unnecessary pauses or filler content, and ensuring that the pace remains engaging. Transitions, whether they be simple fades or more elaborate animated cuts, can help to maintain a smooth flow between different segments of a video, promoting coherence and keeping audiences engaged. Text overlays and graphics can enhance the storytelling by emphasizing key points or adding visual interest. In the ever-evolving landscape of YouTube, effective editing not only assists in crafting a polished final product but also allows creators to adapt quickly to changing viewer preferences and trends. By mastering these editing techniques, aspiring YouTubers position themselves to attract and retain subscribers, ultimately cultivating a loyal audience base that fuels their journey toward success.

VII. EDITING YOUR VIDEOS

A crucial aspect of any successful YouTube venture is the art of editing videos effectively. Editing shapes the narrative, enhances visual appeal, and ensures a polished final product that can engage viewers more deeply. By cutting unnecessary footage, adding transitions, and incorporating background music, creators can enhance the storytelling aspect of their videos. The strategic use of edits can invoke emotions and maintain viewer interest; this is particularly vital given the short attention spans prevalent in today's digital landscape. Elevating production quality through thoughtful editing not only improves viewer experience but also signals professionalism, which can be pivotal in attracting and retaining subscribers.

Engaging content requires a balance between substance and style, and this is where editing serves as a powerful tool. Utilizing software that offers a variety of features—such as color correction, text overlays, and sound editing—can significantly affect the overall impact of a video. Color grading can create a specific atmosphere, from vibrant energy to somber tones, influencing how viewers interpret the content. Embedding graphics and animations can help to emphasize key points, making the material more digestible. Creators should remain mindful, however, to avoid over-editing, which can detract from authenticity. Finding that sweet spot where professional editing meets genuine expression is essential for developing a loyal audience. Meticulous editing not only enhances technical aspects but also aligns with a creator's brand identity. This consistency in style serves to establish a recognizable presence on the platform, fostering a deeper connection with the audience. Being attentive to community feedback regarding editing choices can inform future projects and illustrate a commitment to improving content. Regularly assessing the effectiveness of editing techniques against viewer retention statistics can empower creators to refine their approach, mitigate mistakes, and capitalize on successful elements. In sum, editing is not simply a post-production task; it is an integral part of the creative process that deserves careful consideration in the pursuit of YouTube stardom.

CHOOSING EDITING SOFTWARE

Selecting the appropriate editing software is vital in shaping the quality and impact of your YouTube content. A myriad of options exists, each varying in complexity, features, and usability levels. For beginners, user-friendly programs like iMovie or Filmora offer intuitive interfaces and essential editing tools that facilitate a smoother creative process. These platforms allow users to master the basics, such as cutting, transitions, and audio synchronization, without overwhelming them with advanced features. On the other hand, aspiring creators keen on producing high-quality content might consider more sophisticated software like Adobe Premiere Pro or Final Cut Pro. While these programs have steeper learning curves, they unlock a wealth of functionalities, including advanced color grading, motion graphics, and multi-camera editing, which can significantly enhance the visual appeal of your videos.

Making an informed choice among these software options requires a careful assessment of your specific needs as a content creator. Considerations such as budget, intended video quality, and desired features play pivotal roles in determining which software will serve you best. While some options come with one-time purchase prices, others operate on subscription models, requiring ongoing financial commitment. In addition to financial factors, reflect on your long-term goals; if your ambition is to scale your channel and establish a distinct brand identity, investing in professional-grade software from the outset may yield better returns. Exploring trial versions can provide valuable insight into the user experience and capabilities, ensuring that the software aligns with your creative vision and technical proficiency. The editing software you choose not only affects the production quality of your videos but also influences your creative workflow. A well-selected program can streamline the editing process, allowing you to focus on storytelling and engagement rather than technical hindrances. As you become more comfortable with your chosen software, consider investing time into tutorials and online courses that can further enhance your skills. Engaging with online communities and forums can also provide support and tips that contribute to a more productive editing experience. In the fast-paced world of YouTube, a seamless editing process is essential; the right software empowers creators to maintain consistency, ensuring that their content remains appealing and relevant to their audience, ultimately aiding in the quest to achieve substantial subscriber growth.

EDITING STYLES AND TECHNIQUES

When delving into the realm of editing styles and techniques, the distinction between various approaches becomes pivotal in elevating a YouTube channel's appeal. Each content creator possesses a unique voice, which should harmonize seamlessly with their editing style. Creators might utilize jump cuts for a dynamic pacing that keeps viewers engaged or opt for a more narrative-driven approach with longer takes, providing a sense of immersion. Each technique carries its own emotional weight, influencing how the audience perceives the content. Creators must remain attuned to their target demographics preferences, as tailoring editing styles to audience expectations can foster a deeper connection and enhance overall engagement. Crafting an individual style requires experimentation and adaptation, anchoring the creators identity within the vast landscape of YouTube. Effective use of editing techniques can enhance storytelling by manipulating visual and audio elements to guide viewer perception. Incorporating sound effects, background music, and visual transitions can create a compelling atmosphere that captivates audiences. The strategic placement of music can evoke a particular emotion, whether it's excitement or nostalgia, while sound effects can punctuate jokes or emphasize action. Text overlays and graphics can serve to underscore key messages or provide supplementary information, helping to contextualize the narrative. These techniques not only enrich the viewing experience but also enable creators to convey their ideas more effectively. By meticulously refining these elements, creators can produce videos that foster an immersive atmosphere, encouraging viewers to return for more, thus aiding in the growth of their subscriber base.

The ongoing evolution within digital media necessitates that creators remain flexible in their editing strategies. Adapting to current trends in editing, such as the rising popularity of those dramatic changes seen in TikTok-style videos—often characterized by quick shifts, engaging hooks, and bold visual choices—

can significantly affect a YouTube channels performance. Understanding platform-specific features, such as YouTubes Shorts capability, also allows for innovative formats that can attract attention and drive engagement. Continuous learning about emerging editing software and techniques equips creators with the tools necessary to diversify their content and keep their audience engaged. Embracing change not only empowers creators to maintain relevance but also enables them to stand out in a saturated market, ultimately paving the way towards attaining millions of subscribers.

ADDING MUSIC AND SOUND EFFECTS

In the realm of digital storytelling, sound plays an essential role in enhancing the viewers experience, working harmoniously with visuals to evoke emotion and maintain engagement. Music, for instance, can set the tone of a video, whether it be upbeat and energizing or somber and reflective. Sound effects contribute an additional layer of immersion, providing auditory cues that complement the on-screen action. Creators must judiciously select and synchronize these auditory elements, as an inappropriate choice can disrupt the flow and confuse the viewer. A well-timed sound effect can punctuate a moment, drawing attention to a significant event, while background music can help establish pacing, ultimately facilitating an emotional connection with the audience. Thus, the thoughtful integration of music and sound effects becomes a pivotal component in crafting a compelling narrative that resonates with viewers.

It is crucial to consider copyright issues when adding audio elements to video content. Utilizing royalty-free music and sound effects—not only supports the creative process but also safeguards against potential legal ramifications. Platforms like YouTube provide libraries of licensed audio that can enhance videos without the worry of copyright infringement. Failing to adhere to copyright laws can result in video takedowns or even channel demonetization, which undermines the creators ability to reach a broader audience and generate income. In this sense, the strategic choice of sound elements not only enriches the emotional palette of a video but simultaneously protects the creators investment of time and energy into their channel. An understanding of licensing and the use of original or properly licensed audio is a critical aspect of sound design that cannot be overlooked. Incorporating music and sound effects strengthens a creator's brand, showcasing a distinctive style that can differentiate them from competitors. Consistency in audio elements—such as signature sounds or theme music—creates a recognizable auditory identity, fostering a sense of familiarity and loyalty among viewers. This familiarity can heighten brand recall, encouraging subscribers to return and engage with new content. Crafting a unique soundscape not only enhances the viewing experience but also underscores a creators personal brand narrative. As content creators navigate their journeys on YouTube, embracing the power of sound as a narrative tool can elevate their videos from mere visual experiences to fully immersive storytelling endeavors, laying the groundwork for enduring subscriber relationships and channel growth.

VIII. THUMBNAILS AND TITLES

An impactful visual presence on YouTube hinges significantly on the strategic use of thumbnails and titles. These elements serve as the first point of interaction between the creator and the potential viewer, necessitating a calculated approach that marries creativity with clarity. Thumbnails should be designed to evoke curiosity while clearly reflecting the content of the video. High-resolution images with bold and contrasting colors can enhance visibility across a myriad of devices, ensuring that the thumbnail stands out in crowded feeds. Likewise, incorporating text or graphic elements that hint at the videos value proposition can further entice clicks, bridging the gap between the thumbnail and the viewer's initial interest in the content.

Equally important is the crafting of titles that not only capture attention but also optimize searchability. Effective titles should be concise yet descriptive, integrating keywords that potential viewers are likely to search for. This alignment with YouTubes algorithm enhances discoverability, directly influencing the video's reach and engagement. Titles can convey a sense of urgency or exclusivity—phrases such as You Won't Believe or Must Watch can catalyze viewer action by creating psychological triggers. A well-formulated title paired with a captivating thumbnail synergizes to maximize the video's initial traction, pivotal for converting casual browsers into loyal subscribers.

The interplay between thumbnails and titles should reflect the personality and theme of the channel to build a consistent brand identity. As viewers begin to associate particular visual styles and language with a creator, the potential for establishing a dedicated audience increases substantially. This consistency lays the groundwork for viewer retention and fosters a sense of community amongst subscribers. In an environment where numerous creators vie for viewers' attention, those who effectively curate their visual branding through thoughtful thumbnails and compelling titles are more likely to stand out and achieve lasting success. Consequently, mastery of these elements is a foundational strategy for any determined YouTube creator aiming to scale their audience and impact.

IMPORTANCE OF THUMBNAILS

In the competitive landscape of YouTube, the visual presentation of content often dictates initial viewer engagement. Thumbnails play a critical role in this aspect, serving as the first impression a potential viewer encounters. An eye-catching thumbnail can compel viewers to click on a video amidst countless others, thereby increasing visibility and potential audience reach. With the average viewer scrolling through many options, a well-designed thumbnail with vibrant colors, clear text, and striking imagery can create a strong call to action. This visual appeal becomes the distinguishing factor, making it essential for beginners and seasoned creators alike to invest time in designing thumbnails that not only attract but also accurately represent the video's content.

Beyond aesthetics, thumbnails also function as a vital means of conveying the essence of the video. A creator must be adept at balancing creativity with clarity to ensure that the thumbnail effectively communicates the subject matter without misleading potential viewers. This strategic representation builds viewer expectations and sets the tone for the content that follows. Consistent branding in thumbnails fosters recognition, enabling followers to easily identify a creators videos amidst the multitude of uploads on the platform. Thus, the consistency in style can enhance viewer loyalty, as subscribers come to associate specific visual cues with quality content, which reinforces the overall brand identity. The impact of thumbnails extends to algorithmic considerations that influence video performance. YouTube's algorithms favor videos with high click-through rates—an outcome largely driven by compelling thumbnails. When a videos thumbnail successfully attracts viewers, it not only boosts immediate engagement but also contributes to long-term visibility within the platforms recommendation systems. Investing in thumbnail design is not merely an artistic endeavor; it is a strategic approach that can significantly influence a creators growth trajectory. By harnessing the power of enticing thumbnails, creators position themselves not just for initial viewer engagement, but for sustained success as part of a comprehensive strategy to achieve millions of subscribers over time.

CREATING CLICK-WORTHY TITLES

Successful content creators undeniably understand that the first impression a viewer receives is often encapsulated in the title of a video. A click-worthy title serves as a gateway, enticing viewers to engage and compelling them to click through to the content. To craft such titles, creators must strike a balance between intrigue and clarity, ensuring that the title accurately reflects the content while simultaneously piquing curiosity. Effective techniques include using powerful, evocative language, incorporating compelling numbers or statistics, and posing thought-provoking questions. Titles that promise valuable information or entertainment resonate well with viewers, making them more likely to engage with the content. Leveraging keywords is essential in creating impactful titles that align with search engine optimization (SEO) practices. By incorporating relevant keywords into titles, creators can significantly enhance their visibility on both YouTube and external search engines. These keywords should be strategically placed, ideally towards the beginning to capture attention quickly. Analyzing existing popular content in the same niche can provide insights into trending keywords and themes that resonate with target audiences. Incorporating emotional triggers in titles—such as words that evoke curiosity, humor, or urgency—can amplify the likelihood of clicks. The effectiveness of a title is often measured not just by the number of clicks it garners but also by the audience it attracts, ensuring that viewers find what they were promised. Testing and iterating on titles can play a crucial role in refining this essential aspect of content creation. A/B testing different title variations can help identify which resonates most deeply with audiences by analyzing engagement metrics such as click-through rates and retention time. Content creators should consider making adjustments based on viewer feedback or performance data, allowing them to remain responsive to audience preferences. Assessing competition and observing successful channels can yield innovative ideas that inspire unique title crafting strategies. By consistently evaluating and enhancing their approach, YouTubers can create a repertoire of click-worthy titles that not only foster initial engagement but also build a loyal subscriber base over time. Through these strategies, creators can elevate their content and maximize their impact in a crowded marketplace, laying the groundwork for long-term success.

A/B TESTING THUMBNAILS AND TITLES

In the digital landscape of video content creation, capturing the viewers' attention within the first few seconds is paramount. This urgency underscores the significance of A/B testing thumbnails and titles, crucial elements that greatly influence click-through rates. By experimenting with different visuals and wording, creators can analyze which combinations resonate most with their audience. A bright and colorful thumbnail may attract clicks, while a more straightforward, text-based design might appeal to viewers seeking clarity. Implementing systematic testing allows creators to gather empirical data about viewer preferences, empowering them to craft enticing visuals and titles that succeed in amplifying their reach and engagement.

The methodology behind A/B testing involves not only the creation of alternative thumbnails and titles but also the careful monitoring of performance metrics. Crucial to this process are factors such as viewer retention, engagement time, and audience feedback, all of which provide insights into the preferences of a target demographic. By utilizing A/B testing, content creators can pinpoint which elements in their approach lead to higher viewer satisfaction and interaction. This data-driven decision-making process transforms content strategy from guesswork into a science, fostering a deeper connection with the audience. Over time, these strategies contribute to an evolving understanding of what works best, ultimately driving subscriptions and viewer loyalty. As trends on YouTube shift, so too must the strategies employed by creators, reinforcing the need for continual reassessment of thumbnails and titles. Recent studies have indicated that video titles with a sense of urgency or exclusivity compel users to click, while aesthetically appealing thumbnails can significantly change viewer behavior. Refining these elements not only enhances the immediate appeal of a video but also contributes to long-term brand identity. Creators who embrace A/B testing as an integral part of their content development process typically find themselves more capable of adapting to changing viewer preferences and platform algorithms. In an ever-competitive arena, those willing to iterate and innovate through testing are often the ones who achieve substantial growth and sustained success.

IX. UNDERSTANDING YOUTUBE ALGORITHMS

Navigating the complexities of algorithmic recommendations is essential for aspiring YouTube creators aiming for substantial subscriber growth. At its core, YouTube's algorithm is designed to promote content that engages viewers and keeps them on the platform longer. The algorithm primarily considers user engagement metrics such as watch time, likes, comments, and shares to determine which videos appear in search results or recommended feeds. Understanding this framework allows creators to produce content that aligns with user preferences, thereby enhancing discoverability. By focusing on these key performance indicators, creators can fine-tune their approach, ensuring that each video not only attracts initial views but also encourages viewers to explore additional content, ultimately fostering a loyal subscriber base.

Creating content that resonates with audiences is, therefore, not merely an art but also a science rooted in algorithmic understanding. Video titles, descriptions, and tags play significant roles in how content is categorized and served to potential viewers, making optimizing these elements a critical tactic for growth. Incorporating relevant keywords that a target audience is likely to search for can dramatically boost a videos visibility. Strategic thumbnails and engaging opening sequences are pivotal in capturing viewer attention quickly. These techniques are essential for combatting the competition, as countless videos vie for viewer attention each day. The marriage of creativity with algorithmic insight positions talented creators to capitalize on trending topics and viewer interests, establishing a dynamic channel that evolves with audience demands.

In this continually evolving landscape, adaptability remains key to long-term success on YouTube. The platform frequently updates its algorithm, reflecting shifts in user behavior and technological advancements. Creators who monitor these changes and adjust their strategies accordingly are more likely to sustain and grow their subscriber base. Responding to shifts toward shorter content formats, as evidenced by the rise of YouTube Shorts, can enable creators to reach new demographics and engage viewers effectively. Leveraging analytics to monitor viewer engagement patterns can inform when and how to release new content, maximizing its impact. This iterative process of learning and adaptation not only empowers creators to refine their craft but also cultivates resilience, ensuring they remain relevant in an increasingly competitive market.

HOW THE ALGORITHM WORKS

At the heart of YouTube's functionality lies a multifaceted algorithm designed to maximize user engagement and content discovery. This algorithm operates through a complex interplay of data points, including user behavior, video engagement metrics, and content relevance. When a user interacts with content—be it through likes, shares, comments, or views—the algorithm takes note of these actions to personalize future recommendations. By analyzing historical user data, the algorithm evolves to present videos that not only align with the viewers past preferences but also introduce viewers to new creators who may resonate with their interests. This system of personalized content delivery is anchored in machine learning, which continuously refines its predictive abilities based on ever-growing datasets.

Understanding how to optimize content for this intricate algorithm is critical for creators seeking to expand their reach. Properly crafting video titles, descriptions, and tags using relevant keywords can significantly enhance discoverability. Trying to align content with trending topics or search terms can also offer a strategic advantage. Engagement is further boosted through captivating thumbnails and compelling intros that hook viewers within the first few seconds. Importantly, creators should monitor analytics to identify what works; metrics such as audience retention rates and click-through rates provide valuable insights into viewer preferences. Adapting content based on these insights not only informs future videos but allows for a more responsive approach to audience interests.

A creator's ability to navigate changes in the algorithm can set them apart in an increasingly competitive landscape. As algorithms evolve, staying informed about updates and best practices becomes paramount. Building a consistent upload schedule, engaging with viewer comments, and fostering community interaction are essential tactics to increase visibility over time. Regularly assessing channel analytics helps creators adapt their strategies in real-time, ensuring that they remain relevant amidst shifting trends. Over the long term, combining an understanding of the algorithm with quality content and active engagement fosters a sustainable growth trajectory, enabling creators to not only attract but retain a passionate subscriber base.

FACTORS AFFECTING VIDEO RANKING

Engagement metrics play a pivotal role in determining how videos rank on YouTube. The algorithm takes into account various forms of user interaction, including likes, comments, shares, and watch time. High levels of engagement signal to YouTube that a video is resonating with viewers, thus prompting the platform to promote it more aggressively within search results and recommendations. Content creators can enhance these metrics by creating compelling thumbnails and titles that capture attention and encourage clicks. Ending videos with a call to action, such as requesting viewers to comment or share, can further boost engagement rates. By understanding that engagement is not just a goal but a vital component of ranking, creators can tailor their content strategies to foster a deeper connection with their audience. Another significant factor influencing video ranking is search engine optimization (SEO). Just as traditional web pages utilize keywords to improve their visibility in search results, YouTube videos benefit from effective keyword usage to attract relevant viewers. This includes optimizing video titles, descriptions, and tags with strategic keywords that potential viewers are likely to search. Structuring content to address specific questions or topics can enhance its relevance, thus increasing the likelihood of appearing in search results. Video transcriptions also serve as a useful tool, providing text that can be indexed by search engines and helping viewers find content more easily. By integrating SEO best practices, content creators can significantly amplify their videos discoverability and ensure it reaches a wider audience. Consistency in content delivery cannot be overstated when considering video ranking dynamics. The YouTube algorithm favors channels that post regularly and maintain a predictable upload schedule. This consistency not only builds anticipation among subscribers but also establishes a routine that can drive viewership over time. Creators who commit to a content calendar are better positioned to analyze trends, experiment with various content types, and adapt their strategies based on audience feedback and performance metrics. Regular uploads can enhance viewer retention and encourage subscribers to engage more actively with the channel. As a result, consistency shapes not only viewer habits but also signals to YouTube that a channel is an authoritative source in its niche, bolstering its ranking in search results and recommendations.

STRATEGIES TO WORK WITH THE ALGORITHM

Understanding the intricacies of YouTubes algorithm is essential for any creator aiming to thrive on the platform. At its core, the algorithm prioritizes viewer engagement—considering factors like watch time, likes, comments, and shares. Creating high-quality content that captivates viewers from the outset is fundamental. Engaging thumbnails and compelling titles can draw potential viewers in, but maintaining their interest throughout the video is crucial for maximizing watch time. It is beneficial to employ storytelling techniques, pacing, and visual elements that resonate with the target audience. By consistently analyzing which videos perform better in terms of audience retention and engagement, creators can continually refine their approach, ensuring that they align their content strategies with algorithmic preferences. Regularly updating and optimizing content is another powerful strategy creators can employ to work harmoniously with YouTubes algorithm. Over time, trends on the platform evolve, and topics that may have resonated previously may fall out of favor. Staying abreast of current trends and adjusting content accordingly can help maintain relevance. Leveraging data analytics tools available on YouTube can provide insights into audience demographics, viewing habits, and engagement metrics. By dissecting this information, creators can strategize future content that not only meets viewer preferences but also adheres to algorithmic inclinations. This proactive approach requires diligence but ultimately fosters an adaptive content creation cycle that is more likely to yield growth in subscribers.

Collaborative efforts between creators can also serve as a strategic avenue for leveraging the algorithm to one's advantage. Partnering with other content creators allows for cross-promotion, exposing channels to new audiences and providing a fresh perspective to existing viewers. When creators collaborate, they can combine their unique styles and audiences, which boosts viewer engagement and can lead to increased visibility across the platform. Featuring guest appearances or shout-outs can help build community within the creator ecosystem, further promoting viewer retention and interaction—a critical aspect the algorithm rewards. By fostering collaborations, creators not only enhance their own visibility but also contribute to a vibrant and interconnected YouTube environment, essential for sustained success.

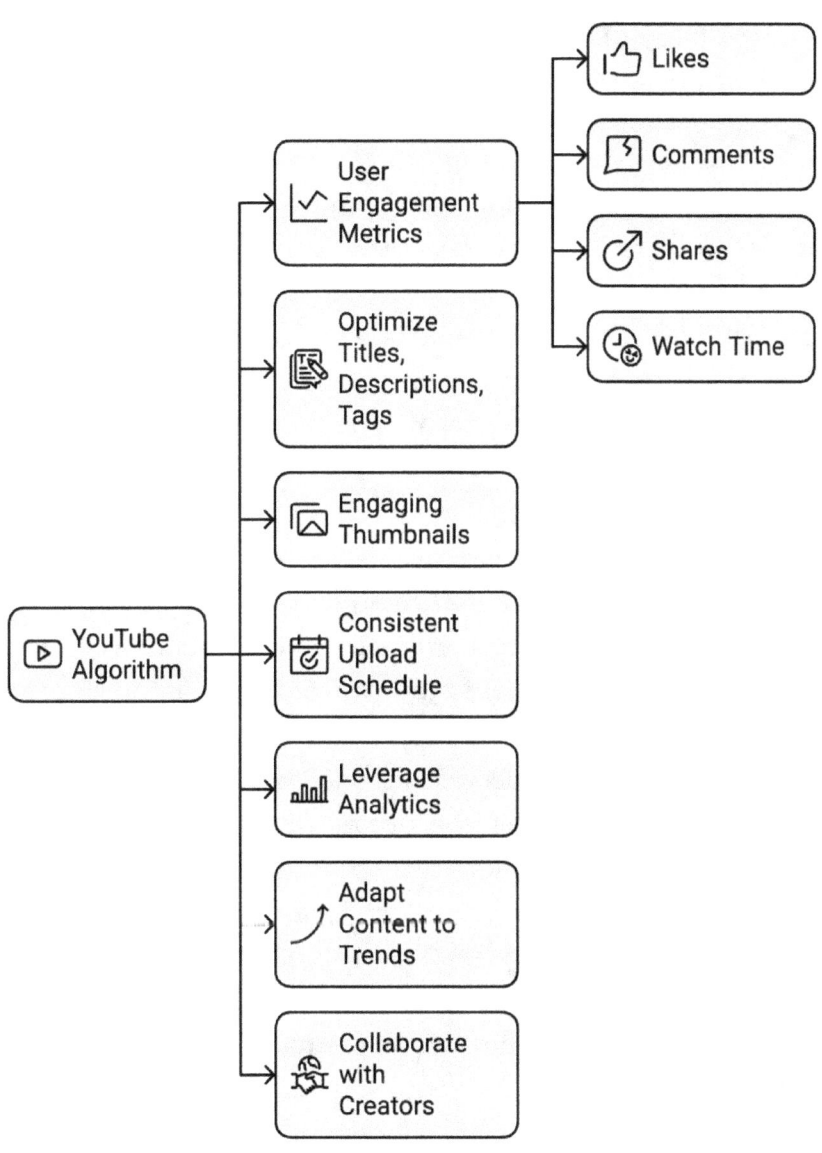

X. OPTIMIZING VIDEO DESCRIPTIONS

A well-crafted video description is an essential component of any successful YouTube strategy, serving as both a promotional tool and a means to enhance discoverability. Effective descriptions leverage relevant keywords that align with the anticipated search queries of the target audience, which directly influences the video's ranking within YouTube's algorithm. By integrating terms and phrases commonly associated with the video content in a natural and engaging manner, creators can increase their visibility and attract more viewers. Providing metadata, such as timestamps for significant points within the video, enhances user experience and encourages viewer retention, as audiences can navigate content more efficiently. The strategic use of keywords and metadata transforms video descriptions from mere summaries into potent tools that attract and inform potential viewers. Beyond keyword optimization, video descriptions should also embody a persuasive and engaging narrative that prompts viewers to watch the content. The opening lines must capture attention immediately, offering a compelling hook that outlines the value of the video. As viewers skim descriptions, a direct invitation to engage—whether through comments, shares, or subscriptions—can foster a sense of community and increase interaction rates. Including links to related videos, playlists, and social media handles can create interconnected pathways for viewers, encouraging deeper engagement with the creators content. This approach not only enhances the chances of retaining viewers' attention but also facilitates brand loyalty, as audiences are more inclined to subscribe when they perceive ongoing value from a creator.

Revisiting and revising video descriptions regularly can yield significant dividends in maintaining viewer interest and optimizing for changing algorithms. As trends shift and audience preferences evolve, creators should analyze the performance of their descriptions using analytics to identify which elements resonate most effectively with viewers. Implementing A/B testing for different description styles or keyword selections can also pinpoint what drives engagement and increases reach. By remaining adaptable, creators can refine their strategies to align with both platform updates and viewer expectations. In this iterative process, optimizing video descriptions not only supports growth in terms of views and subscriptions but also reinforces a creator's commitment to delivering valuable, audience-focused content.

IMPORTANCE OF DESCRIPTIONS

Effective engagement with an audience hinges significantly on the descriptions that accompany video content. These descriptions act as a mini-summary, providing potential viewers with a glimpse of what to expect. Well-crafted descriptions not only enhance the searchability of a video through the strategic inclusion of keywords but also set the tone and context, which can compel users to click. By outlining the video's content with clarity, creators can effectively convey the value proposition, enticing viewers who are browsing for relevant topics. An informative and engaging description acts as the first point of interaction with potential subscribers, thereby significantly influencing click-through rates and initial viewer interest.

In the bustling ecosystem of YouTube, standing out requires more than just attractive thumbnails and intriguing titles; it necessitates leveraging every opportunity to communicate with the audience. Detailed descriptions give creators a robust platform to elaborate on the video's themes, providing insight that can enrich the viewing experience. Including relevant links, credits, or additional resources within the description not only offers viewers more ways to engage but also fosters a sense of community and trust. This practice heightens user retention, encouraging viewers to explore more of the creators content. Thus, descriptions serve as an essential tool in branding and viewer retention strategies.

The role of descriptions transcends mere functionality; they contribute to storytelling and brand identity. A well-written description can evoke emotion, elucidate key messages, and invite viewer interaction, which can cultivate a loyal subscriber base. As content creators hone their skills, refining their descriptive techniques can lead to significant improvements in metrics such as watch time and subscriber growth. Each aspect of a description—tone, language, and structure—should resonate with the creators audience, reflecting their voice and intent. A compelling description can differentiate a channel in a crowded space, reinforcing the creators mission while aiding in the viewer's journey toward deeper engagement.

KEYWORD RESEARCH AND USAGE

The strategic selection and deployment of keywords can fundamentally alter the trajectory of a YouTube channels visibility. By integrating relevant keywords within titles, descriptions, and tags, content creators can significantly enhance their videos discoverability in search results and recommendations. This is not merely about inserting popular terms but about understanding the intent behind them. Successful creators often utilize tools like Google Trends, TubeBuddy, and VidIQ to conduct in-depth research, revealing the phrases their target audience is actively seeking. Armed with this knowledge, creators can craft content that not only addresses these queries but also positions their videos favorably within search algorithms. Thus, keyword research is not just a technical exercise; it embodies a nuanced understanding of audience behavior and market demands.

Effective keyword usage extends beyond the mechanics of searchability; it plays an essential role in shaping content strategy. Creators should form an interconnected web of related keywords to build a cohesive narrative throughout their videos and channels. A cooking channel might focus on keywords surrounding particular cuisines, dietary restrictions, or cooking techniques, creating playlists that cater to these interests. By consistently aligning content with researched keywords, creators establish authority in specific niches, encouraging subscribers to expect and seek out their unique perspective. As YouTube algorithms favor user engagement, strategically placed keywords can enhance viewer retention by ensuring that content remains relevant and resonates with audience expectations.

Mastering keyword research and usage is a continuous cycle of analysis and adaptation. As trends shift and audiences evolve, creators must remain vigilant, reassessing their keyword strategies and integrating new, impactful terms into their content. Regularly revisiting analytics provides invaluable insights into viewer demographics and engagement patterns, allowing for an iterative approach to keyword selection. Community engagement, through comments and social media, can uncover emerging interests that have not yet been widely captured. By remaining agile and responsive to these changes, content creators not only boost their visibility but also foster deeper connections with their audience, thus ensuring sustainable growth in an ever-competitive landscape.

CALLS TO ACTION IN DESCRIPTIONS

An effective call to action (CTA) within video descriptions serves as a critical bridge between captivating content and audience engagement. The language used in these descriptions should evoke a sense of urgency or importance, prompting viewers to take specific steps after watching the video. Phrases such as "Subscribe now for more content like this" or "Join the community in the comments below" can create an interactive atmosphere. By strategically placing CTAs at the beginning and end of the descriptions, creators encourage viewers not only to reflect on the content but also to participate in a broader dialogue around it. This method bolsters viewer retention and fosters a sense of belonging, essential components of a successful YouTube channel. Incorporating compelling CTAs also aligns closely with YouTube's algorithm, which rewards engagement metrics such as likes, comments, and subscriptions. When creators effectively invite viewers to act, they increase the likelihood of these engagement markers. A well-placed prompt encouraging viewers to share their thoughts on a specific topic can lead to a flurry of comments, signaling to the algorithm that the video resonates with its audience. This relationship underscores the importance of understanding both content creation and optimization in today's competitive landscape. The careful construction of CTAs within descriptions, informed by data and user behavior, not only directs viewer actions but also strategically enhances the likelihood of wider visibility within the platform.

The efficacy of CTAs in video descriptions is further magnified when they are seamlessly integrated with overall content strategy. Creators should tailor their CTAs to reflect the themes and messages of their videos, ensuring that they feel organic rather than forced. This alignment not only fosters authenticity but also bolsters viewer trust, encouraging long-term loyalty to the channel. Analytics can be leveraged to evaluate the performance of different CTAs, allowing creators to refine their approaches based on what resonates best with their audience. By cultivating a dynamic interplay between content, viewer interaction, and responsive CTAs, channels can elevate their engagement levels, ultimately propelling them toward subscriber milestones and sustained growth.

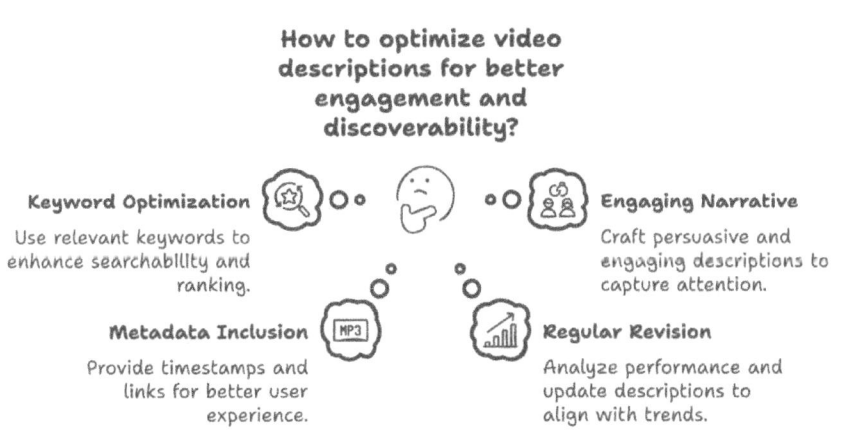

XI. ENGAGING WITH YOUR AUDIENCE

Building a strong connection with viewers goes beyond mere entertainment; it encapsulates the creation of a community where audience members feel valued and understood. Content creators who prioritize engagement often see their channels flourish, as they invite conversation through comments, live streams, and social media interactions. By acknowledging viewers input and responding to their feedback, creators can cultivate a sense of loyalty and belonging, which keeps audiences returning for more. Leveraging features like polls and questions allows creators to gauge what content resonates most, fostering a two-way dialogue that enhances the viewer experience. This level of engagement creates a dynamic atmosphere around the channel, enabling content to evolve in ways that align closely with audience preferences.

In addition to direct engagement, incorporating storytelling elements into videos can significantly enhance viewer connection. Narratives present authentic experiences that resonate on a personal level, inviting viewers to see themselves within the story. Creators who infuse storytelling into their content often find that it captivates audiences, drawing them deeper into the material while simultaneously encouraging sharing and discussion. Crafting a compelling arc—complete with relatable characters, challenges, and resolutions—enables creators to evoke emotional responses, transforming casual viewers into loyal fans. This emotional investment not only retains subscribers but also encourages word-of-mouth growth, as viewers feel compelled to share impactful stories with their networks. The interplay of quality content and audience engagement can dramatically influence a creator's visibility on the platform. YouTube's algorithm rewards channels that demonstrate high levels of interaction through watch time, likes, and shares, which makes audience engagement an essential component of any growth strategy. Creators should monitor analytics carefully to identify which types of content elicit the most engagement, using this data to inform future videos. Consistently high engagement rates can result in better recommendations from the platform, leading to wider exposure and potentially viral success. By establishing a cycle of producing engaging content and actively participating in viewer interactions, creators can harness audience enthusiasm to propel their channels to new heights.

RESPONDING TO COMMENTS

Engagement is a vital component in the evolution of any successful YouTube channel, and responding to comments plays a crucial role in fostering a vibrant community. When creators actively engage with their audience by responding to comments, they not only cultivate loyalty among their subscribers but also encourage more viewers to participate in discussions. Personalized responses to comments demonstrate that the creator values input from their audience, making subscribers feel recognized and connected to the content. This dynamic not only helps to humanize the creator but also facilitates a two-way conversation, turning passive viewers into active participants. Each interaction can significantly enhance the overall viewer experience, which is essential for long-term retention and subscriber growth. Responding to comments provides content creators with a unique opportunity for audience feedback. Comments often contain valuable insights regarding what viewers enjoyed, what they wish to see more of, or areas that need improvement. By analyzing this feedback, creators can tailor their content to better align with their audiences preferences, thereby increasing viewer satisfaction and retention. Addressing constructive criticism also portrays a sense of professionalism and willingness to adapt, which can further engender trust in the creator's brand. Close attention to audience suggestions can lead to innovative content ideas that resonate deeply, enhancing the overall quality of the channel. In this regard, effective commenting not only serves as a form of engagement but as a vital tool in the ongoing content creation process.

The tone and substance of responses can significantly influence the surrounding community's atmosphere. Creators who take the time to craft thoughtful, respectful replies cultivate a positive environment that can deter negativity and trolling. By setting a standard for constructive dialogue, creators can instill a sense of safety and respect within their comment sections, leading to a more enjoyable experience for all participants. This positivity can create a ripple effect, encouraging viewers to engage more positively with one another. In responding to comments, creators must be mindful of their language and demeanor, as these elements shape the community culture. A well-nurtured comment section not only reflects the creators values but importantly signals to potential subscribers that the channel is a welcoming space, further contributing to its growth and success.

CREATING COMMUNITY POSTS

Engagement within the community plays a pivotal role in the

success of a YouTube channel, and one effective method to foster such engagement is through community posts. These posts allow creators to interact with their audience beyond video content, offering a space to share updates, solicit feedback, or initiate discussions. By consistently sharing polls, behind-the-scenes insights, or even personal anecdotes, creators can establish a closer connection with their viewers. This personal touch not only humanizes the content creator but also encourages subscribers to feel invested in the channel's trajectory. Engaging with the community is essential, as it helps to maintain viewer loyalty and encourages viewers to become vocal advocates for the brand, thus amplifying reach and engagement.

The strategic incorporation of community posts can provide valuable insights into audience preferences and behavior. Regularly posting polls or asking for input on upcoming content ideas allows creators to gauge what resonates most with their audience. This feedback loop not only informs content creation but enhances viewer satisfaction by ensuring the material aligns with subscriber interests. Creators can leverage community posts to promote upcoming videos or events, effectively driving traffic to their main content. By treating their audience as collaborators rather than mere consumers, creators can harness this interactive feature to sustain enthusiasm and investment, resulting in a more dedicated and proactive subscriber base.

The potential for viral growth through effective community post strategies should not be overlooked. Engaging and shareable posts can reach beyond traditional subscriber metrics, attracting new viewers who may not have encountered the channel otherwise. A well-crafted humorous post or a poignant question may encourage likes and shares across various social media platforms, leading to organic discovery and expanded audience reach. It is crucial for creators to approach these posts with creativity and authenticity to resonate with both existing and potential subscribers. By integrating community posts into their broader content strategy, creators can unlock new avenues for connection and visibility that contribute significantly to their growth on the platform. Community posts represent not merely a supplementary tool but a vital component in the overarching strategy for building a successful YouTube presence.

HOSTING LIVE Q&A SESSIONS

Engaging directly with an audience can significantly amplify a YouTube creator's reach and relevance, a potential unlocked through live Q&A sessions. These events provide a unique platform for creators to connect personally with their viewers, fostering a sense of community that recorded videos simply cannot replicate. The interactive nature of live sessions allows for real-time feedback and discussion, enhancing viewer loyalty and encouraging participation. Creators often notice that such direct engagement increases the emotional investment of their audience, which can lead to higher retention rates and improved subscriber growth. This immediate communication channel can also reveal insights about audience preferences and expectations, enabling creators to tailor future content more effectively. Preparing for a live Q&A requires not only technical readiness but also an understanding of audience dynamics. Successful creators often promote their sessions in advance, utilizing social media channels and community posts to hype the event and gather questions. During the session, having a structured format—such as a shot list or a sequence of topics—can help maintain focus, making the experience enjoyable for both the creator and the audience. Responding thoughtfully to viewer questions demonstrates genuine interest and care, essential elements in cultivating a loyal follower base. Creators should also be flexible and willing to adapt, as spontaneous discussions can often lead to the most engaging content.

Post-session evaluation is another critical aspect that cannot be overlooked. Creators should analyze audience reactions and the types of questions that generated the most engagement to inform future content strategies. This analysis allows for iterative improvements in quality and relevance, directly impacting subscriber growth. Incorporating highlights from the Q&A into edited videos can extend the reach of valuable discussions beyond the live audience, offering content that resonates with viewers who may have missed the event. By treating live Q&A sessions not merely as standalone events but as integral components of a wider content strategy, creators can maximize their impact and deepen their connection with their audience, ultimately driving further growth in their YouTube journey.

XII. PROMOTING YOUR VIDEOS

Engaging with potential viewers often requires a multifaceted marketing approach that transcends merely uploading content to YouTube. One effective strategy is leveraging social media platforms to amplify reach and drive traffic to video content. By sharing teasers, behind-the-scenes clips, or even promotional images on platforms like Instagram, Twitter, and TikTok, creators can pique interest and encourage cross-platform engagement. Tailoring the message to target audiences on each platform helps solidify the creators brand identity while fostering a sense of community. Utilizing analytics tools to identify peak engagement times can enhance the timing of these posts, ensuring that content reaches its audience when they are most active. Establishing a robust online presence that resonates with the audience will not only attract new viewers but also create a loyal following that eagerly anticipates future uploads.

Collaboration with other content creators stands out as a powerful technique for expanding a videos reach and exposure. Forming partnerships with creators who share a similar audience allows for a mutually beneficial exchange that can draw new subscribers to both channels. Joint projects, live streams, or guest appearances can introduce creators to one another's audiences in an authentic way, leveraging their respective strengths and unique voices. Co-created content often harnesses diverse perspectives and creative ideas, resulting in videos that are richer and more engaging. Both collaborators should promote the resulting content across their channels, encouraging their followers to explore and subscribe to the other's work. This not only builds a sense of camaraderie within the creator community but also enhances both parties visibility, contributing to sustained growth in subscriber numbers.

Consistency and strategic planning are paramount for successful video promotion, as they establish a routine that viewers come to rely on. Developing a content calendar can streamline the production process while ensuring a steady flow of uploads that adheres to a regularly spaced schedule. Viewers appreciate predictability, as it fosters anticipation for upcoming videos and encourages them to return. Once a schedule is in place, it is crucial to engage with the audience through comments and community posts, creating a dialogue that nurtures viewer loyalty. Engaging with this feedback not only fosters a deeper connection with subscribers but also allows creators to adapt their content based on viewer preferences and trends. Over time, this commitment to consistency and audience engagement cultivates a dynamic channel ecosystem that supports ongoing growth and encourages a vibrant community of subscribers.

SOCIAL MEDIA MARKETING STRATEGIES

An effective approach to enhancing visibility on YouTube involves leveraging various social media platforms to create a cohesive marketing strategy. By promoting video content across platforms such as Instagram, Facebook, and Twitter, creators can reach diverse audiences and drive traffic to their YouTube channel. Engaging with followers through regular posts, stories, and live sessions expands brand awareness and fosters community involvement. This interconnectedness not only amplifies the presence of the YouTube channel but also creates opportunities for collaborations and cross-promotions with other content creators. By developing tailored content that resonates with the specific user demographics of different platforms, marketers can cultivate a loyal following that translates viewership into subscriptions and interactions on YouTube.

To maximize the effectiveness of social media marketing strategies, consistency and frequency in posting must be emphasized. Establishing a regular schedule helps in building anticipation among audiences; followers are more likely to stay engaged when they know when to expect new content. Utilizing analytics tools available on various social media platforms can provide invaluable insights into audience preferences, optimal posting times, and trending topics. Creators should craft messages that encourage shares and interactions, employing call-to-action techniques that resonate with the unique cultures of each platform. This kind of deliberate strategy not only boosts engagement but also enhances the potential for organic growth across platforms, directly influencing the visibility and reach of the YouTube channel itself.

Adaptability is critical in the ever-changing landscape of social media marketing. As platforms frequently update their algorithms and features, content creators must remain vigilant and responsive to these shifts. Staying informed about emerging trends or new functionalities allows marketers to pivot their strategies effectively, ensuring that they capitalize on opportunities for increased engagement. Experimenting with various content formats, such as polls, challenges, or even behind-the-scenes glimpses, keeps audiences intrigued and invested in the brand. By embracing a mindset of continual learning and adjustment, YouTube creators can refine their social media marketing tactics, ultimately guiding their journey from initial obscurity to mainstream recognition and subscriber growth. This dynamic approach not only enhances audience retention but also establishes a solid foundation for sustained success in digital marketing efforts.

COLLABORATIONS WITH OTHER CREATORS

Connecting with fellow content creators opens numerous avenues for both growth and innovation on platforms like YouTube. By collaborating with others, creators tap into diverse audiences, effectively broadening their reach while fostering a sense of community. This mutual exchange can take various forms, from guest appearances in videos to joint projects that bring together distinctive styles and perspectives. Such collaborations often invigorate a channel, adding fresh energy and ideas that may appeal to existing subscribers while attracting new viewers intrigued by the collaboration. These partnerships can help creators pool their resources, share expertise, and cultivate relationships that lead to future opportunities, cementing their positions within the ecosystem of content creation.

Successful collaborations hinge on the synergy between creators, aligning their visions and values to produce cohesive and engaging content. A thoughtful approach is essential; mismatched styles may alienate audiences rather than unite them. Prior to collaborating, creators should assess each other's content quality, audience engagement, and overall branding to ensure compatibility. Detailed planning is crucial, as setting clear goals for the partnership can enhance the final outputs effectiveness. This strategic alignment allows creators to define their unique offerings, whether that's humor, information, or artistic execution, thereby ensuring that the collaboration resonates qualitatively with both audiences. Reviews and feedback from each creators community can provide essential insights for refining collaborative efforts in the future.

Collaboration also serves as a powerful tool for creative inspiration, sparking new ideas that may not have emerged in isolation. Interacting with fellow creators exposes individuals to different techniques, narratives, and production styles, encouraging experimentation and growth. This creative synergy can result in innovative content formats that captivate audiences in unique ways, thereby enhancing the overall quality of the channel. Successful YouTube creators frequently share that their best ideas often arise from brainstorming sessions and collaborative discussions. The act of working together fosters an environment of support and encouragement, which can be invaluable given the challenges inherent in content creation. By engaging in thoughtful collaborations, creators can significantly amplify their impact, ensuring sustained growth and relevance in the ever-evolving landscape of digital media.

PAID ADVERTISING OPTIONS

Leveraging paid advertising options is a strategic way to boost visibility and accelerate growth on YouTube. For creators looking to gain traction quickly, platforms such as Google Ads offer targeted advertising solutions that can position videos in front of specific demographics, interests, or behaviors. These paid advertisements can manifest in various formats, including in-stream ads that play before popular videos, display ads that appear alongside video content, and overlay ads that provide a more subtle prompt to viewers. The advantage of these options lies in the ability to fine-tune campaigns based on performance metrics, ensuring that content reaches the ideal audience. This data-driven approach not only increases brand awareness but also drives user engagement, prompting viewers to subscribe and participate in the channel.

Another potent avenue for paid advertisements is influencer partnerships. Collaborating with established YouTubers or social media influencers can effectively amplify reach and credibility. By partnering with creators whose audience aligns with your target demographic, the potential for converting viewers into subscribers increases significantly. These collaborations often involve sponsored content where the influencer promotes your channel or specific videos within their existing audience. This form of advertising can harness the trust that influencers have built with their viewers, directly translating into increased visibility for your brand. This strategy can offer insights into audience behavior and preferences, enabling you to refine your content approach and optimize future advertising investments.

Utilizing retargeting campaigns can create a compelling cycle of engagement and subscriber growth. Retargeting involves targeting users who have previously interacted with your videos or channel, reminding them of your content and enticing them to return. This technique can be particularly effective as it focuses on an audience already familiar with your brand, increasing the likelihood of conversion. Implementing retargeting ads on platforms like YouTube and across social media can facilitate continuous visibility, reinforcing viewer interest and prompting actions such as subscriptions or video shares. With careful analysis and strategic implementation, these paid advertising options become essential tools in a comprehensive marketing plan, enhancing the ability to forge a loyal audience and maximize the channels growth potential.

XIII. ANALYZING VIDEO PERFORMANCE

Understanding audience engagement metrics is fundamental to assessing the overall performance of video content. Engagement metrics such as watch time, likes, comments, and shares provide a comprehensive view of how viewers interact with the video. Analyzing these elements allows creators to discern which aspects of their content resonate most with their audience. A spike in comments may indicate that a particular topic sparked interest and encouraged dialogue, while a high watch time signifies that viewers were captivated enough to remain through the entirety of the video. By dissecting these interactions, creators can glean insights into audience preferences and tailor future content accordingly, enhancing the likelihood of increased engagement and retention.

The role of the YouTube algorithm cannot be underestimated in the landscape of video performance analysis. This complex algorithm determines video visibility, utilizing user behavior data to influence recommendations. Creators who wish to optimize their performance must take into account not only how well their videos perform independently but also how they fit into broader trends and viewer behavior on the platform. Key factors include the use of relevant keywords in titles and descriptions, effective thumbnail designs, and timely content releases that align with what audiences are actively seeking. By synthesizing performance data with algorithmic insights, creators can strategically position their videos for maximized reach and impact, ensuring their content is not only seen but also appreciated within a crowded digital marketplace.

Regularly reviewing performance analytics allows creators to stay agile and adaptable in an ever-evolving platform landscape. YouTube's dynamic environment necessitates that creators pivot strategies based on real-time data and emerging trends. Metrics such as click-through rates (CTR) on thumbnails and the demographic breakdown of viewers can reveal critical information about what is working and what is not. Armed with this feedback, creators can refine their content strategies, whether that means experimenting with new formats, engaging with comments more consistently, or incorporating trending topics. The ability to analyze and respond to performance effectively positions creators not just to survive but to thrive amidst challenges, ultimately leading to sustained growth in subscriber count and viewer loyalty. Such an iterative approach to content creation and analysis ensures a stronger connection with audiences while fostering a successful trajectory on YouTube.

USING YOUTUBE ANALYTICS

Understanding audience behavior and engagement is paramount for any content creator aiming to achieve significant success on YouTube. YouTube Analytics serves as an invaluable tool for monitoring viewer preferences, offering data-driven insights into which videos resonate most with audiences. By examining metrics such as watch time, average view duration, and retention rates, creators can identify trends and patterns that inform content strategy. If a particular video garners unusually high engagement, analyzing its elements—such as title, thumbnails, and content format—can reveal what captivated viewers. This strategic approach not only enhances future productions but also fosters greater connection with the audience, ultimately nurturing a more loyal subscriber base.

Demographic data provided by YouTube Analytics grants creators an essential understanding of their audience composition. Insights into viewers' geographic locations, age groups, and gender offer a nuanced view that can tailor content to specific segments. If analytics reveal a sizable portion of the audience is composed of teenagers, creators might pivot their messaging or references to align with the interests and culture of that demographic. Such targeted adjustments can significantly boost engagement and subscriber growth, reflecting the importance of adapting to audience shifts. Consistent analysis can uncover opportunities for collaboration with other creators, broadening reach and attracting new subscribers from different viewer bases. The role of YouTube Analytics extends beyond mere observation; it becomes a proactive strategy in a creators growth journey. The ability to track the impact of particular changes—like varying posting times or experimenting with different content types—empowers users to iterate and refine their approach continually. Using A/B testing for thumbnails or titles can lead to higher click-through rates, while monitoring subscribers gained or lost during specific periods reveals the effectiveness of content drops or marketing efforts. This iterative process, grounded in analytics, encourages creators to develop a dynamic and responsive channel. Harnessing these analytical insights not only helps creators visualize their growth trajectory but equips them with the knowledge necessary to execute informed strategies that drive long-term success on the platform.

KEY METRICS TO TRACK

Fostering an understanding of audience engagement is paramount for any YouTube creator aspiring to grow their channel. Metrics such as watch time and audience retention rate provide essential insights into how well content resonates with viewers. Watch time, or the total minutes users spend viewing videos, stands as a direct indicator of a channels performance within YouTubes algorithm. A high watch time not only improves visibility in searches but also suggests that viewers find the content appealing enough to stay engaged. Audience retention, on the other hand, measures the percentage of a video that viewers watch on average. By tracking this metric, creators can identify specific points within their videos where interest wanes, allowing for more precise targeting of content adjustments. If there's a significant drop-off after a particular segment, it might indicate the need for tighter editing or more captivating storytelling techniques. In addition to engagement metrics, the analysis of subscriber growth provides a clear picture of a channels overall health and potential for expansion. Tracking the rate at which subscribers are gained or lost over time can reveal trends that inform content strategy. A spike in subscribers, for example, may correlate with a specific video or a change in content strategy, suggesting effective approaches worth replicating. Conversely, a decline in subscribers can serve as a crucial warning sign; creators might need to reconsider their contents relevance to their audience. Analyzing the source of subscriber growth—with insights about whether viewers come from suggested videos, search results, or external links—can assist in fine-tuning promotional efforts across various platforms, thereby broadening reach and engagement efforts.

Equally vital is monitoring the performance of individual videos through key metrics such as likes, comments, and shares. These indicators serve not only as an affirmation of the content's quality and viewer satisfaction but also play a significant role in how videos are promoted within YouTubes ecosystem. A video that garners high engagement rates generally signals to the algorithm that the content is worthwhile, thus improving its chances of being recommended to new viewers. The interaction in the form of comments can provide direct feedback, offering valuable insights into viewer preferences and thoughts on what they'd like to see in the future. By cultivating a robust understanding of these metrics, creators can strategize effectively, promoting sustained growth and a loyal subscriber base, while continuously refining their content to meet the evolving demands of their audience.

ADJUSTING STRATEGIES BASED ON DATA

In the dynamic realm of YouTube, responsiveness to analytics is paramount. Analytics tools provide a wealth of information, including viewer demographics, watch time, and engagement rates. By meticulously examining these metrics, creators can identify patterns and preferences among their audiences. If data indicates that a particular video format garners higher retention rates, producers can replicate that format in future projects. Conversely, content that fails to resonate can be re-evaluated or adapted to better align with viewer interests. Adjusting strategies based on data not only enhances content relevance but also fosters a deeper connection with the audience, ensuring that creators remain competitive in an ever-evolving landscape. Building upon insights gleaned from analytics, creators must also embrace an iterative approach to their content strategy. This involves continuously testing new ideas and formats, measuring their success through systematic data analysis. Each piece of content serves as both an artistic endeavor and a scientific experiment, offering valuable feedback on what captivates audiences. Testing varied thumbnail designs or titles can yield significant differences in click-through rates. By observing these metrics and making informed adjustments, creators can streamline their production process to amplify audience engagement. This process encourages innovation while simultaneously honing in on effective strategies, thus ensuring that each new release builds upon the successes of the last.

Fostering adaptability in response to shifting trends and viewer feedback is essential for sustained growth on YouTube. The platform itself often undergoes significant changes, from algorithm updates to new features. Successful creators remain vigilant and ready to pivot their strategies as needed. This flexibility allows for quick corrections based on unique data points, such as abrupt changes in audience behavior or the introduction of emerging content genres. Engaging with the audience through comments and community posts can provide qualitative data that further informs content direction. An effective YouTube strategy hinges not only on initial planning but also on the continuous refinement and recalibration of approaches based on real-time insights, ensuring creators can thrive amidst ongoing change.

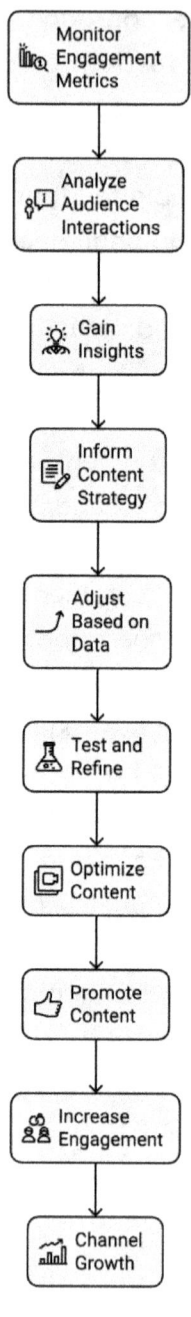

XIV. MONETIZATION OPTIONS

As content creators cultivate their YouTube channels, understanding potential revenue streams becomes crucial for achieving sustainable growth. Ad revenue established through YouTubes Partner Program remains a primary monetization method, allowing creators to earn from their video views. Successful monetization often transcends this method. Creators are encouraged to explore affiliate marketing, where they promote products or services and earn a commission on sales generated through their referral links. This approach aligns well with many content niches, as it allows creators to recommend products they genuinely believe in, fostering authenticity and trust with their audience. Diversifying income streams, in this instance, can elevate a creators financial stability and reduce dependency on a single source. Beyond traditional monetization methods, merchandise sales have emerged as a powerful tool for creators to connect with their audience while generating revenue. Developing branded merchandise not only incentivizes fans to engage with the creator on a deeper level but also enhances their personal brand equity. Successful channels leverage platforms like Teespring or Printful to produce custom products that resonate with their audience, further embedding themselves into their fans' lives. This approach does not solely rely on transactional interactions; it creates a sense of community as fans proudly wear or use their favorite creator's goods. Thus, the intersection of branding and e-commerce can significantly drive revenue while deepening the creator-viewer relationship.
Content creators can tap into the lucrative domain of sponsor-

ships and brand partnerships to bolster their monetization strategy. As brand marketing increasingly shifts towards influencer collaborations, YouTubers with established audiences can secure sponsorship deals that provide substantial financial compensation. By carefully selecting partnerships that align with their content and audience values, creators can maintain their authenticity while reaping the benefits of brand collaborations. Engaging in strategic partnerships not only enhances a channels revenue potential but also opens avenues for cross-promotion, exposing creators to broader audiences. By diversifying monetization avenues through ad revenue, merchandise, and sponsorships, creators position themselves for growth in an ever-competitive digital landscape, ensuring their continued relevance and financial success.

YOUTUBE PARTNER PROGRAM

To access the full range of monetization opportunities on the platform, creators must navigate the prerequisites of the program carefully. The YouTube Partner Program (YPP) requires channels to meet specific eligibility criteria, which includes amassing at least 1,000 subscribers and achieving 4,000 watch hours within the last twelve months. These requirements are designed to ensure that only dedicated content creators who can genuinely engage audiences are allowed to monetize their content. As a result, aspiring YouTubers must focus not only on quantity but also on the quality of their content, as captivating videos tend to keep viewers engaged longer, directly contributing to meeting these milestones. This essential step underscores the correlation between audience retention and prospective monetization, emphasizing the importance of strategic content planning and execution.

Once creators unlock the YouTube Partner Program, a world of monetization options becomes available, including ad revenue, channel memberships, and merchandise shelf integration. Ad revenues, which stem from displaying ads before, during, or after videos, significantly contribute to a creators income; however, it is crucial to understand that the amount earned can vary based on several factors, including viewer demographics and engagement rates. Channel memberships allow loyal fans to support creators directly in exchange for exclusive perks, fostering a tighter community and encouraging sustained engagement. By diversifying revenue streams, creators can establish a more stable financial foundation for their channel, minimizing dependence on any single income source. This multi-faceted approach to monetization not only enhances the creators financial well-being but also reinforces the creators relationship with the audience. Participation in the YouTube Partner Program opens doors to invaluable analytics and support resources, enabling creators to optimize their strategies effectively. Creators can access insights about viewer demographics, engagement rates, and traffic sources, empowering them to refine their content to better resonate with their target audience. Armed with this data, creators can identify trends, tailor their content strategies, and leverage successful influencer marketing tactics. YPP members typically receive priority support from YouTube, which can be essential for navigating challenges or understanding policy changes. This combination of data analytics and personalized assistance ultimately enhances the capacity of creators to adapt to platform changes and continue producing relevant, engaging content—factors that are crucial for long-term success in a dynamic digital landscape.

SPONSORSHIPS AND BRAND DEALS

Building a successful YouTube channel often culminates in the pursuit of sponsorships and brand deals, which can significantly enhance both the credibility and profitability of a creators platform. These partnerships typically arise when brands identify a synergy between their values and the creators audience engagement. The strategic alignment allows both parties to benefit from shared visibility—brands can tap into the creators loyal follower base, while creators can gain financial support and access to products that resonate with their content. A well-executed sponsorship not only bolsters the creators income but also lends an added layer of authenticity to the content, provided that the collaboration feels genuine and enriches the viewing experience. Navigating the landscape of sponsorships demands careful consideration and professionalism. Creators must prioritize transparency and authenticity when partnering with brands; failing to do so can alienate viewers who value trust and connection with their favorite content creators. Establishing clear terms and communicating openly with potential sponsors about audience demographics, engagement metrics, and content style can foster a mutually beneficial relationship. Turning down offers that do not align with one's personal brand or audience interests is crucial for maintaining integrity. This discerning approach helps in cultivating long-term partnerships that add value to the channel, rather than short-lived arrangements that could compromise credibility.

Successful sponsorships can serve as a significant catalyst for growth, opening doors to higher visibility and further brand collaborations. As creators engage with brands that resonate with their audience, they not only diversify their income streams but also enrich their content through unique products or services integrated seamlessly into their videos. Leveraging analytics tools to assess audience reception to sponsored content can provide valuable insights for future partnerships and content development. Thus, creators should view sponsorships not merely as financial arrangements but as integral components of their growth strategy, reinforcing their brand identity while enhancing viewer engagement and satisfaction.

MERCHANDISING AND AFFILIATE MARKETING

Building an effective merchandising strategy is pivotal for YouTube creators aiming to expand their revenue streams. When leveraged correctly, merchandise becomes a tangible extension of a creator's brand, allowing fans to connect on a deeper level. Successful YouTubers often design products that resonate directly with their audience, whether it's apparel featuring catchphrases, bespoke artwork, or themed accessories. The key lies in understanding the audiences preferences and aiming for quality over quantity. By showcasing merchandise in entertaining and engaging ways, such as through unboxing videos or behind-the-scenes snippets, creators can foster a sense of exclusivity and community around their brand. This integration not only encourages loyalty among existing fans but also attracts new viewers, enhancing both subscriber numbers and potential sales. In parallel with merchandising, affiliate marketing serves as another powerful strategy for creators seeking to monetize their platforms. This approach involves promoting products or services to their audience, generating commission-based revenue from sales made through shared links or unique promo codes. The successful implementation of affiliate marketing demands authenticity; followers are more likely to make purchases if they believe in the creators sincerity regarding the products. By selecting affiliate partnerships that align with their content and values, creators can maintain their image while diversifying their income. A beauty YouTuber may collaborate with skincare brands, while a gaming channel might endorse gaming peripherals. Providing thorough, honest product reviews alongside affiliate links not only empowers viewers to make informed decisions but also reinforces the creator's role as a trusted source in their niche. Engaging in both merchandising and affiliate marketing requires an astute understanding of audience behavior and preferences. Creators must remain attentive to shifts in interests, potential market trends, and the evolving landscape of consumer preferences. This fluidity demands ongoing interaction with the audience through comments, surveys, and social media engagement to gauge their evolving tastes. By being receptive to feedback and willing to adapt their offerings, creators can ensure a consistent relevance that drives sales and subscriber growth. Effective use of analytics tools can provide insights into which products resonate most with different segments of the audience, allowing for tailored marketing strategies. Merging these two strategies not only boosts revenue but also cultivates a loyal subscriber base eager to support a brand they feel connected to.

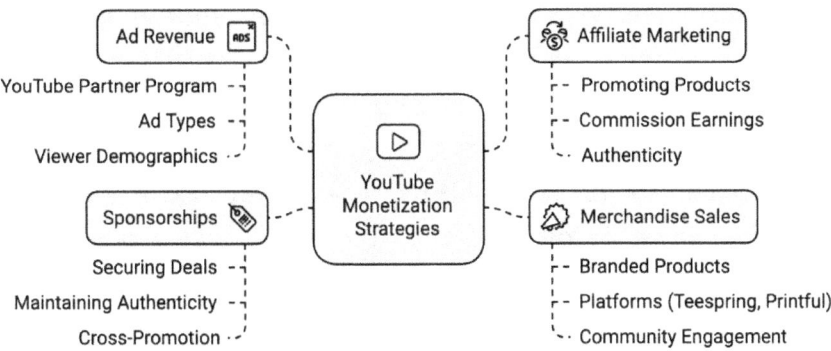

XV. BUILDING A COMMUNITY

Fostering a sense of belonging is essential for any YouTube creator aiming to build a robust community around their channel. When viewers feel connected, they are more likely to engage with content, share it, and return for more. Creators can cultivate this connection by actively interacting with their audience through comments, live chats, and social media platforms. Encouraging viewer participation by asking questions, inviting feedback, and even featuring user-generated content not only enhances viewer loyalty but also creates an open dialogue that enriches the community experience. This engagement transforms passive viewers into active participants, thereby deepening their investment in the content and its creator.

Establishing trust plays a pivotal role in the process of community building. Authenticity is crucial; creators who share their personal journeys, successes, and even failures are more relatable to their audience. By being transparent about their experiences, creators invite viewers into their world, fostering an atmosphere of mutual respect and understanding. This trust is further reinforced by consistent content quality and schedule. When viewers know they can expect reliable and valuable content, they develop a sense of security that reinforces their loyalty. In this way, trust becomes the cornerstone of a healthy YouTube community, allowing it to flourish organically as subscribers feel supported and appreciated.

The impact of a thriving community extends beyond individual creators and can significantly influence a channels growth trajectory. As engaged audience members share content within their networks, they serve as ambassadors for the brand, broadening its reach organically. Active communities are often more willing to support their favorite creators through subscriptions or merchandise purchases, enhancing monetization efforts. A strong community can provide valuable insights and ideas for future content, ensuring that creators consistently deliver material that resonates with their viewers interests. Building a community is not merely a strategy for growth; it is a foundational element that fosters sustainability and long-term success on YouTube, enabling channels to evolve alongside their audience.

CREATING A LOYAL FANBASE

Cultivating a loyal fanbase necessitates more than just producing high-quality content; it requires creators to engage meaningfully with their audience. Building a genuine connection can be achieved through consistent interaction, whether that involves responding to comments, hosting live Q&A sessions, or acknowledging feedback in future videos. By fostering a sense of community, creators transform passive viewers into active participants, making them feel valued and integral to the channels growth. This community-building approach enhances viewer loyalty, as fans are more likely to stick around and advocate for a creator when they feel a personal connection. Sharing personal anecdotes or experiences can create relatable content that resonates deeply with an audience, further solidifying loyalty and encouraging subscribers to actively participate in discussions. Establishing a unique brand identity can also significantly bolster a creators ability to cultivate a devoted following. Effective branding goes beyond visuals; it encapsulates the creator's values, personality, and storytelling style, thus setting them apart in a saturated marketplace. This identity should permeate all content, creating a cohesive experience that allows viewers to easily recognize and distinguish the channel. Implementing consistent themes, catchphrases, or visual elements not only enhances recall but also reinforces the connection between the creator and their audience. Strategizing branding efforts based on audience demographics ensures that content speaks directly to their interests and preferences. An authentic brand fosters trust, encouraging viewers to remain loyal and recruit others to the channel, thereby expanding the fanbase further.

The journey to create a loyal fanbase requires ongoing adaptation and responsiveness to viewer trends and platform dynamics. Staying attuned to feedback and analytics can provide insights into what resonates and which areas need improvement. Creators should utilize data analytics to analyze viewer retention rates, popular content themes, and viewers demographic profiles, allowing for informed adjustments to content strategy. Embracing new trends or formats, whether through collaborations or leveraging cross-platform opportunities, can expand reach and engagement. An adaptive approach ensures that the channel remains relevant and continues to foster excitement among subscribers, effectively transforming fleeting viewership into sustained loyalty. By engaging with their audience, developing a distinct brand, and being adaptable to change, creators can build a devoted community that grows organically over time.

ENGAGING WITH FANS OFF-PLATFORM

Establishing connections with fans outside of YouTube plays a pivotal role in a creators long-term success. Engaging audiences through various social media platforms such as Instagram, Twitter, and TikTok allows creators to showcase their personalities beyond the confines of video content. These platforms serve as venues for spontaneous interactions, where fans can directly communicate with creators, fostering a sense of community. By posting behind-the-scenes content, personal stories, or responding to fan inquiries, creators can deepen their relationship with viewers, ensuring that they feel seen and valued. This emotionally charged connection can translate into increased loyalty and heightened engagement, encouraging fans to become more active participants in the creators journey.

Diversifying content across multiple platforms also serves a strategic purpose. Each social media channel has its unique audience, and tailoring content to fit these varied demographics enables creators to reach a broader spectrum of potential fans. Short and engaging video clips on platforms like TikTok can captivate a younger audience, while detailed analyses and discussions can thrive on platforms such as Twitter. By understanding the nuances of each platform, creators can optimize their messaging and content delivery, ultimately driving traffic back to their YouTube channel. This approach not only boosts visibility but also creates opportunities for cross-promotion, where creators can link back to their YouTube videos in their posts, effectively funneling their off-platform audience to their main content hub. The ability to engage with fans off-platform is not merely about promoting content; it's about cultivating a brand that resonates on a personal level. Creators should focus on authenticity, as fans increasingly seek genuine connections with those they support. Utilizing tools such as newsletters or fan clubs can facilitate deeper connections and create a sense of exclusivity, making fans feel part of an inner circle. Hosting events—whether virtual meetups, Q&A sessions, or live streams—can enhance this rapport further, allowing creators to interact with fans in real-time. By investing in these relationships outside of YouTube, creators can build a dedicated and enthusiastic fanbase that not only consumes their content but actively champions their work across platforms and communities.

HOSTING EVENTS AND MEETUPS

Networking plays a pivotal role in the journey of a YouTube creator, and hosting events and meetups presents a unique opportunity to cultivate such connections. Engaging with fellow creators, industry professionals, and avid viewers in a live setting can foster collaboration and significantly enhance a creators visibility. These gatherings serve as platforms for sharing insights, experiences, and best practices, which can ultimately lead to fruitful partnerships. In-person interactions allow for a genuine exchange of ideas, cultivating a sense of community that is often lost in the digital realm. By organizing events, creators not only elevate their own personal brands but also contribute to a broader ecosystem where knowledge and creativity can flourish, promoting growth for all participants involved.

These meetups can be strategically designed to cater to specific niches or themes, aligning closely with a creators content. By carefully selecting guest speakers or panelists who resonate with their audience, creators can enhance their brand identity while also providing significant value to attendees. Workshops or Q&A sessions can encourage audience participation, creating memorable experiences that linger long after the event concludes. This level of engagement can help solidify a creators status as an authority in their field, attracting even more viewers and subscribers. These events can be recorded and shared across various platforms, maximizing exposure and further amplifying the creators reach. Consequently, the multi-dimensional benefits of hosting events provide a practical avenue for enhancing a creators reputation and subscriber count in an increasingly saturated market.

The logistics of organizing events may seem daunting, but careful planning can lead to tremendous rewards. From selecting an appropriate venue to managing ticket sales and promotions, each aspect must be meticulously considered to ensure a successful outcome. Collaborating with local businesses, securing sponsorships, or leveraging online platforms can mitigate costs and enhance the experience for attendees. Utilizing social media and online communities for promotion can help creators reach a broader audience beyond their existing subscriber base. Importantly, post-event follow-ups are crucial; sharing content from the event and expressing gratitude to participants can further strengthen relationships and maintain engagement long after the gathering. Hosting events and meetups not only enriches the creators journey but also lays the groundwork for sustained growth, ultimately helping to transition from a novice with zero subscribers to a recognized figure with millions.

XVI. STAYING CONSISTENT

The commitment to a regular posting schedule is integral to cultivating a sustainable YouTube channel. Audiences thrive on anticipation; when viewers know when to expect new content, their engagement levels soar. This reliability fosters a sense of community and investment among subscribers, giving them a reason to return regularly and interact with each new video. Maintaining a consistent posting schedule demands careful planning and discipline, both of which are crucial for managing content creation and other responsibilities. Creators who employ calendars to delineate production timelines often find that setting clear, achievable goals helps them remain focused and motivated. As each posting deadline approaches, this structure can mitigate the potential for burnout, allowing creators to produce quality content while also maintaining their personal livelihoods. The algorithms that govern YouTube's recommendation system reward consistency, making it an essential component of long-term success. Regular uploads signal to the algorithm that a channel is active and deserving of promotion, potentially exposing content to a broader audience. This creates a symbiotic relationship where creators benefit from more reach, and viewers receive fresh content more frequently. Mere frequency is not sufficient; each video must still uphold quality standards to maintain viewer retention. As viewers develop a relationship with a creator's style and messaging, any deviation from this established norm can lead to disengagement. Thus, the balance between frequency and quality becomes paramount. By staying consistent without sacrificing the integrity of the content, creators can navigate the complex dynamics of audience expectations and algorithmic preferences, thriving in an increasingly crowded marketplace.

Adaptability in the quest for consistency can greatly enhance a creators ability to connect with their audience. The digital landscape is perpetually evolving, necessitating that content creators remain flexible in their strategies and approaches. While consistency is vital, it should not come at the cost of innovation and responsiveness to viewer interests. Regularly analyzing engagement metrics can reveal shifts in viewer preferences, guiding creators to modify their content in ways that resonate more profoundly. This adaptability fosters greater viewer loyalty, as subscribers appreciate a creators willingness to consider feedback and experiment with new formats or topics. By harmonizing a consistent posting schedule with a receptive and agile creative process, YouTube creators can build enduring subscriber relationships while continually evolving to meet the demands of their audience. This dynamic interplay underscores the broader truth that staying consistent is not solely a matter of frequency, but also one of relevance and connection.

IMPORTANCE OF REGULAR UPLOADS

Consistency in content creation is essential for cultivating a loyal audience on platforms such as YouTube. When viewers know what to expect—and when to expect it—they are more likely to return to the channel regularly. Establishing a clear upload schedule not only helps in retaining viewer attention but also builds anticipation among subscribers. This habitual engagement is akin to a ritual, as followers come to look forward to new content on specific days, creating an ever-deepening connection between the creator and the audience. Regular uploads help to solidify this relationship, transforming casual viewers into devoted fans who are invested in the channels growth and success, further amplifying community interactions in the comments section, which can, in turn, lead to increased visibility through YouTube's algorithms.

Beyond fostering audience loyalty, consistent uploads significantly impact channel visibility, which is vital for growth. YouTube's algorithm favors channels that provide regular content, actively pushing such videos to a wider audience. By uploading frequently, creators enhance their chances of being included in recommended feeds and search results, which ultimately leads to more views and potential subscribers. This cycle of uploading, gaining visibility, and attracting new users feeds into itself, creating a momentum that can catapult a channel from obscurity to prominence. Regular content creation allows creators to experiment with different formats and themes, receiving valuable feedback from viewers, which can guide future content strategies. This iterative process means that creators can refine their approach based on audience preferences, making uploads not just a strategy for retention, but also a tool for continuous improvement.

The benefits of maintaining a regular upload schedule extend beyond just audience engagement and visibility; they also provide opportunities for skill development and creative exploration. As creators commit to a consistent routine, they increase their familiarity with the technical aspects of video production, including filming, editing, and post-production processes. This regular practice not only enhances the quality of the content being produced, but it also fosters creative innovation, as creators may feel more liberated to experiment with new ideas and formats. The discipline developed through consistent content creation encourages a growth mindset, as creators learn to navigate challenges related to production and audience reception more effectively. Over time, this dedication not only results in a more polished final product but also contributes to the overall identity and credibility of the YouTube channel, establishing it as a reliable source of entertainment or information that audiences can trust and rely upon.

CREATING A SUSTAINABLE SCHEDULE

Establishing a successful YouTube channel begins with a well-structured schedule that balances content creation, audience engagement, and personal well-being. Content creators must allocate specific time slots for shooting, editing, and uploading videos, ensuring a rhythm that audience members can rely on. This regularity not only helps in maintaining viewer interest but also aligns with YouTubes algorithm, which favors channels that post consistently. A sustainable schedule incorporates time for feedback sessions where creators can assess viewer reactions and engagement metrics. By dedicating hours weekly to this analysis, creators can refine their approach, ensuring that future content remains relevant and appealing. Thus, a strategically planned schedule is crucial for sustaining audience growth and maintaining the creators mental health, as avoiding burnout is essential for long-term success.

Incorporating flexibility into a creators schedule can enhance overall productivity without sacrificing quality. While consistency in posting is vital, the dynamic nature of trends on platforms like YouTube necessitates adaptability. Creators should have a core content calendar but also leave room for spontaneous video ideas that may arise from current events or viral trends. This dual approach allows for both structured growth and the fluidity required to respond to audience interests as they evolve. Time should be allocated for collaborative projects and knowledge-sharing with other creators, which can introduce new perspectives and expand viewership. By creating a schedule that supports both stability and spontaneity, content creators can not only cultivate a loyal audience but also foster a creative environment that celebrates innovation.

Prioritizing personal time and self-care within a content creation schedule is fundamental for sustaining artistic integrity and passion. Creators often underestimate the toll that continuous content production can take on their mental and emotional health. Scheduling regular intervals for rest, leisure, and activities unrelated to the channel fosters a healthier work-life balance and rejuvenates creative energies. This practice not only prevents burnout but also enhances the quality of content produced, as rested creators are more likely to generate fresh ideas and engaging narratives. A sustainable schedule should reflect a holistic approach to life as a content creator, harmonizing the demands of the YouTube platform with the creators personal growth and resilience. By treating their schedule as both a tool for productivity and a framework for well-being, creators can navigate the challenges of the YouTube landscape while thriving as individuals.

BALANCING QUALITY AND QUANTITY

In the competitive landscape of YouTube, the delicate interplay between quality and quantity significantly shapes a content creators journey. While the initial impulse may be to inundate the platform with a barrage of videos, a more strategic approach often yields better long-term results. Content that is meticulously crafted tends to engage viewers more effectively, fostering a loyal community that values the creators unique voice and perspective. This resonance, however, must be balanced with a consistent upload schedule; frequent engagement is essential in maintaining visibility within the algorithmic confines of YouTube. Creators must navigate this juncture by prioritizing impactful content while adhering to a realistic posting frequency that keeps their audience engaged without compromising their creative integrity. The YouTube algorithm rewards regular uploads, which compels creators to find innovative ways to maintain their content output without sacrificing quality. An effective strategy involves creating a content calendar that allows for batch production, ensuring diverse topics are covered while maintaining a cohesive vision. By planning ahead, creators can allocate adequate time for research, scripting, filming, and editing—all crucial elements that contribute to high-quality content. Smart time management also allows creators to engage with their audience through comments and feedback, adding a personal touch that fosters community. This interaction is invaluable, as it helps gauge viewer preferences and inspires future content, striking a harmonious balance between delivering regular videos and ensuring each piece meets a high standard of excellence.

The balance between quality and quantity manifests as a dynamic journey rather than a fixed goal, requiring ongoing assessment and adaptation. As creators grow and evolve, the metrics of success can shift, prompting them to recalibrate their strategies. Emerging trends or viewer feedback might encourage a creator to pivot towards more immediate, high-quality projects or to experiment with formats that require less production time but maintain audience engagement. This adaptability not only enhances a creator's portfolio but also reinvigorates their passion for content creation. In the end, forging a successful career on YouTube involves understanding that both quality and quantity are interdependent; striking an effective equilibrium allows creators to build a sustainable brand that resonates powerfully with their audience.

XVII. ADAPTING TO TRENDS

In a constantly evolving digital landscape, the ability to pivot in response to emerging trends is crucial for content creators aiming to thrive on platforms like YouTube. Observing the rapid shifts in viewer preferences, successful YouTubers often dedicate time to thorough market research, identifying trending topics, themes, and content formats that resonate with their audience. Whether it's a viral challenge, a cultural phenomenon, or a current event, recognizing these trends early and aligning content with audience interests can significantly enhance visibility and engagement. Utilizing tools such as Google Trends, social media analytics, and audience feedback allows creators to remain attuned to what captivates their viewers, enabling them to adapt quickly and maintain relevance in a saturated market.

Innovative content ideas that reflect the latest trends not only attract new subscribers but also reinvigorate existing audiences. A strategic approach to content adaptation involves experimenting with different styles, formats, and narratives. Integrating popular memes or references into videos can forge a connection with viewers who are active in specific online communities. Live streaming and short-form video content, like YouTube Shorts, are increasingly favored by younger audiences. By embracing diverse content formats and creative storytelling techniques, creators can capitalize on these trends, fostering deeper engagement and enhancing the overall subscriber experience. The ability to innovate while staying true to one's unique voice is essential for standing out amid the competition.

Embracing adaptability fosters long-term success and sustainability on YouTube. As algorithms change and viewer habits shift, those who can pivot effectively are more likely to build resilient channels. Engaging with audience feedback and analytics not only informs adjustments to content strategy but also builds a sense of community and loyalty among subscribers. By developing a growth mindset—one that welcomes change and seeks continuous improvement—creators can navigate the complexities of the platform with greater ease. Adapting to trends, therefore, is not merely a reactive measure; it is a proactive strategy that positions creators for ongoing relevance, engagement, and ultimately, growth in their subscriber base.

IDENTIFYING CURRENT TRENDS

In the rapidly evolving landscape of YouTube, staying attuned to current trends is crucial for creators who aspire to expand their subscriber base. Trends often emerge from shifts in consumer behavior, technological advancements, and cultural phenomena. The rise of short-form content, exemplified by the popularity of TikTok and Instagram Reels, has had a profound impact on YouTubes own features, such as YouTube Shorts. Creators who harness these formats can capture the attention of viewers in under a minute, catering to an audience increasingly seeking quick, digestible content. The ability to identify and adapt to these trends not only fosters relevance but significantly enhances the chances of virality, thereby attracting new subscribers eager for the latest, most engaging content.

Equally important is the influence of audience engagement trends on content strategy.

An increasing number of viewers are drawn to resonant narratives and relatable personalities rather than mere informational videos. This shift indicates a desire for authenticity, prompting creators to forge personal connections with their audiences through storytelling and interactive elements such as live streams and Q&A sessions. Emerging creators can leverage this trend by showcasing their genuine experiences and emotions, which can create a sense of community among followers. Engaging in dialogues through comment sections, polls, and social media platforms further cultivates this relationship, encouraging viewer loyalty. As audiences increasingly seek to feel included in the creative process, successful YouTubers will prioritize interaction over one-way communication.

The analytical aspect of identifying trends cannot be overlooked, as data-driven decision-making is essential for sustainable growth. YouTube's algorithm continually evolves, making it imperative for creators to utilize analytics tools to track viewer behavior, preferences, and engagement metrics. By examining which types of content lead to higher watch times, likes, and shares, creators can fine-tune their strategies to align with what resonates most with their audience. Identifying metrics on peak viewing times and demographic insights allows for targeted content scheduling and personalized marketing campaigns. Thus, the synthesis of trending themes, audience engagement strategies, and analytical insights creates a comprehensive approach that empowers creators to not only capture but also maintain and grow their subscriber base effectively in the competitive realm of YouTube.

INTEGRATING TRENDS INTO CONTENT

The ability to recognize and integrate current trends into content creation is essential for any aspiring YouTuber aiming for virality and substantial growth. Staying attuned to shifting viewer preferences and emerging topics can lead to more engaging and relevant content. Content creators should invest time in research and analysis of trending hashtags, viral challenges, and popular themes within their niche. Platforms such as Google Trends and social media analytics tools can provide insights into what is capturing audience attention. By aligning video content with these trends, creators not only enhance their visibility but also position themselves as timely and informed voices within their communities, fostering a deeper connection with their audience. The integration of trends is not merely about mirroring popular content; it also involves infusing personal creativity and perspective into these trending topics. While it's tempting to follow every trend blindly, the most successful creators understand that authenticity is paramount. They expertly weave their unique storytelling styles and expertise into the fabric of current trends, thereby creating a distinct brand identity. This fusion allows creators to stand out amid a saturated market, offering audiences something fresh and memorable. As trends come and go, those who prioritize a personal touch alongside their timely content are more likely to cultivate a loyal subscriber base that values their individuality.

In addition to elevating engagement and enhancing personal branding, integrating trends can drive algorithmic favorability on YouTube. The platform tends to promote videos that align with popular themes, often propelling them onto trending lists or recommended feeds. Creators who strategically embed trending keywords and concepts into their titles, descriptions, and tags improve their chances of reaching broader audiences. this approach requires a careful balance; content should never compromise authenticity solely for the sake of trending. Successful YouTubers recognize that longevity in their channels growth depends on a sustainable approach, marrying trend-awareness with genuine investment in their craft. By doing so, they not only secure short-term visibility but also build a foundation for lasting success in an ever-evolving digital landscape.

STAYING RELEVANT IN A CHANGING LANDSCAPE

Rapid technological advancements and shifting audience preferences necessitate a dynamic approach to content creation. Content creators who remain static risk losing visibility and relevance, as platforms like YouTube constantly evolve in response to user engagement patterns. The algorithm that governs video promotion operates on increasingly sophisticated metrics, prioritizing not just views but also watch time, audience retention, and user interaction. As such, creators must stay informed about algorithm updates and community trends, adjusting their strategies accordingly. By embracing flexibility and a willingness to experiment with new formats—be it short-form videos, live streams, or collaborations—creators can maintain relevance and capitalize on emerging opportunities.

Another integral aspect of staying relevant in a changing landscape is understanding one's audience deeply. Building a loyal following hinges on recognizing and adapting to audience feedback and preferences. Successful creators often utilize social media platforms and community features on YouTube to foster dialogue with their viewers, effectively shaping their content based on direct input. By leveraging data analytics tools to assess viewer demographics and engagement metrics, creators can tailor their content and improve its quality. This approach not only enhances audience satisfaction, but also increases the likelihood of organic growth, as engaged viewers are more likely to share content and attract new subscribers.

The importance of networking and collaboration cannot be understated in the quest to remain relevant. Engaging with other creators or influencers in similar niches facilitates mutual growth and exposes audiences to fresh perspectives and ideas. Strategic collaborations often yield innovative content that resonates with diverse viewer demographics, driving engagement and increasing visibility across multiple channels. Participating in community events and online forums helps creators stay in tune with industry trends and collective challenges. Nurturing these relationships enables creators to adapt and evolve alongside the rapidly changing landscape of digital content, ensuring that they not only survive but thrive in their YouTube endeavors.

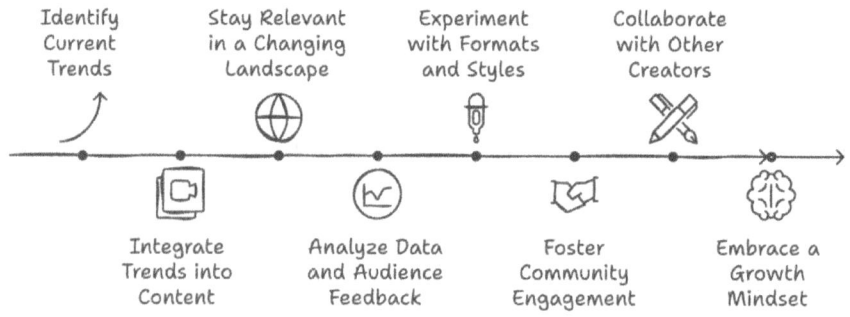

Adapting to Trends for YouTube Success

XVIII. HANDLING CRITICISM AND NEGATIVITY

Navigating the world of online content creation inevitably involves encountering scrutiny and criticism, which can be daunting for even the most resilient individuals. The first step in addressing feedback is to distinguish between constructive criticism and negative attacks. Constructive criticism provides valuable insights that can inform improvements in content quality and audience engagement, allowing creators to enhance their skills and grow their channels. Conversely, negativity that is rooted in trolling or hostility should be recognized as ineffective and dismissed. By developing a clear framework for evaluating feedback, creators can transform the often overwhelming nature of criticism into a manageable and constructive process, leading to personal and professional growth.

Processing criticism requires emotional intelligence and a growth mindset. When faced with negative comments, it is essential to pause and assess one's emotional reactions. Engaging in self-reflection can help creators understand why certain comments trigger emotional responses; this awareness is key to maintaining a positive outlook. Embracing a growth mindset fosters resilience and encourages creators to view criticism as an opportunity for learning rather than a personal attack. Strategies such as seeking peer feedback, engaging in dialogues with supportive communities, and focusing on the positive aspects of well-received content can build confidence in one's abilities, ultimately leading to a strengthened resolve in the face of negativity. Successfully managing negativity involves not only an internal approach but also the implementation of strategies for maintaining online presence. Establishing a clear and engaging social media presence allows for a more controlled narrative surrounding content. Creators should actively respond to their audience, addressing concerns while setting boundaries regarding harmful comments. Building a supportive community cultivates an environment where constructive conversations flourish, reducing the impact of negativity. Regularly celebrating milestones, acknowledging subscriber support, and showcasing behind-the-scenes processes can promote a sense of belonging among followers. By positioning oneself at the center of a positive discourse, creators are more likely to foster resilience and create a sustainable and engaging channel, even amidst the challenges presented by criticism.

RESPONDING TO NEGATIVE COMMENTS

Dealing with criticism is an inherent aspect of content creation, especially on platforms as public and interactive as YouTube. When faced with negative comments, creators must first understand the underlying motivations driving such feedback. Often, negative remarks stem from viewers personal tastes, differing expectations, or even unresolved frustrations. Acknowledging these perspectives can transform how creators perceive criticism. By fostering empathy towards their audience, content creators can better contextualize these comments, viewing them not solely as hostility but as signals indicating areas of improvement or engagement. This shift in mindset promotes resilience, enabling creators to focus on growth rather than succumbing to discouragement. Proactive engagement with negative comments can foster a more positive community environment and potentially turn detractors into advocates. Instead of responding defensively, creators should consider addressing criticism thoughtfully and respectfully. A creator might choose to respond with appreciation for the viewer's honesty while clarifying their intent or content approach. This interaction not only showcases the creators willingness to engage with their audience but also highlights their commitment to improvement. By creating a dialogue, creators can demonstrate to their audience that they are listening and valuing their opinions, which can lead to increased loyalty and trust. The ability to effectively respond to negative comments is instrumental in shaping a creators public persona and can significantly impact their channels trajectory.

Implementing strategies for constructive feedback allows creators to refine their content and presentation. Over time, this iterative process can result in a more authentic and relatable brand, which attracts a wider audience. Embracing criticism can lead to personal growth and professional development, as creators learn to discern valid feedback from unwarranted negativity. By viewing negative comments as opportunities for dialogue rather than attacks on their character, content creators can foster a supportive community that nurtures both their channels success and their personal growth within the ever-evolving landscape of YouTube.

LEARNING FROM CRITICISM

Navigating the complex landscape of online content creation often involves facing criticism that, while initially jarring, can prove to be an invaluable teacher. When aspiring YouTubers receive feedback on their videos, whether positive or negative, it presents an opportunity for self-reflection and growth. Instead of dismissing critical comments or becoming defensive, creators should approach them with an open mind. Analyzing specific points raised by viewers can reveal blind spots in one's content, such as areas lacking clarity or engagement. By actively listening to the audience's perspectives, YouTubers can refine their craft and better cater to their viewers' preferences, ultimately resulting in higher quality content that resonates with a broader audience. Equally important is the ability to differentiate between constructive and destructive criticism. Constructive feedback is often marked by specificity, offering actionable insights into what can be improved, while destructive criticism tends to be vague or negative without offering solutions. Learning to embrace constructive critiques enables creators to focus on tangible improvements, fostering an environment where growth becomes the primary goal. Techniques like summarizing feedback, prioritizing actionable items, and implementing changes in a targeted manner can accelerate the learning process. This disciplined approach not only enhances content quality but also develops resilience in the face of less-than-favorable opinions, equipping creators with the tools to maintain motivation and positivity throughout their journey.

The transformative power of criticism lies in its ability to catalyze personal and professional development. By incorporating feedback into their creative process, YouTubers cultivate a growth mindset that encourages longevity in their careers. Embracing criticism not only leads to refinements in technical aspects, such as video production and editing, but also bolsters the creators personal brand by instilling a sense of authenticity and relatability. As creators adapt their content based on audience input, they foster a stronger connection with their viewers, consequently increasing viewer loyalty and subscriber growth.

In a platform defined by constant change and user feedback, the willingness to learn from criticism can set the stage for sustained success and a thriving YouTube career.

MAINTAINING MENTAL WELL-BEING

Navigating the complex landscape of YouTube can be a rollercoaster of emotions, making it essential for creators to incorporate strategies that support mental well-being. Engaging in the routine of content creation can lead to burnout if not managed properly. Establishing a balanced schedule that includes time for personal reflection, leisure, and connection with others is crucial. To foster resilience, creators should regularly set realistic goals, allowing them to celebrate small victories without becoming overwhelmed by the pressures of chasing viral success. Incorporating mindfulness practices, such as meditation or journaling, can assist in managing stress and maintaining perspective. By prioritizing mental health alongside creative ambitions, content creators can sustain their passion and continue to produce engaging content that resonates with their audience.

Another significant aspect of maintaining mental well-being revolves around community building. Engaging with a supportive network of fellow creators can provide crucial emotional support and foster collaboration opportunities. Social media platforms often serve as extensions of YouTube personalities, allowing for authentic interactions with subscribers and peers. Discerning meaningful connections from mere performative engagement is vital; quality relationships contribute positively to mental health. Participating in forums or content creator events can also offer valuable insights and encouragement, alleviating feelings of isolation common in the digital space. Creators are encouraged to share their challenges and triumphs, promoting a culture that values vulnerability and openness, ultimately leading to stronger bonds and a more fulfilling creative journey.

The significance of self-care cannot be understated when pursuing success on YouTube. Creators must recognize that their mental state influences their content and, by extension, their audience. Practicing self-care involves not just physical health but also nurturing ones emotional and psychological well-being. Regular breaks from filming, engaging in hobbies unrelated to content creation, and seeking professional help when needed can enhance a creators ability to think creatively and innovate. By developing a mindset that prioritizes well-being, creators can minimize anxiety associated with fluctuating subscriber numbers or video performance, thus maintaining a healthier relationship with their craft. Integrating self-care into the pursuit of YouTube success fosters longevity in a competitive environment, allowing creators to thrive both personally and professionally.

XIX. LEGAL AND COPYRIGHT CONSIDERATIONS

Navigating the complex landscape of YouTube requires a keen awareness of legal and copyright considerations, which can profoundly impact a creators success. Content creators must understand that using copyrighted music, images, or video without proper authorization can lead to content strikes, channel demonetization, or even legal action. YouTube employs a robust Content ID system that can detect copyrighted material, resulting in automatic monetization claims or removals. This underscores the importance of originality and obtaining proper licenses when incorporating third-party content into videos. Creators must consider these aspects carefully to safeguard their channels and ensure their production practices adhere to legal standards. In addition to copyright, creators must be mindful of FTC regulations regarding sponsorships and endorsements. Transparency plays a crucial role in maintaining viewer trust; creators are legally required to disclose any paid promotions or product placements prominently. Failure to comply with these regulations can result in penalties and damage to a creators reputation. By fostering honesty with their audience, content creators can build a loyal subscriber base while ensuring compliance with legal frameworks. Thus, integrating ethical practices alongside legal obligations enhances not only a creators standing in the community but also sustains long-term growth and engagement. The importance of understanding fair use cannot be overstated. This legal doctrine permits limited use of copyrighted materials without permission for specific purposes, such as commentary, criticism, or education. For aspiring

YouTubers, grasping the nuances of fair use can be a potent tool for creativity and innovation. Even with fair use, the line can be blurred, making it critical for creators to seek legal counsel when in doubt. By balancing creativity with legal awareness, content creators can carve a niche for themselves while reducing the risk of infringing upon the rights of others. Embedding a strong legal foundation in their creative processes amplifies their ability to thrive on the platform.

UNDERSTANDING COPYRIGHT LAWS

Navigating the complex landscape of content creation on platforms like YouTube necessitates a solid understanding of copyright laws. Creators must be acutely aware of the potential consequences of using copyrighted material, as violations can lead to punitive actions, including video takedowns and channel strikes. Fair use, a doctrine that allows for limited use of copyrighted material without permission, provides a framework for certain types of commentary, criticism, education, and parody. Determining what constitutes fair use can often be murky, as it relies on a case-by-case analysis, considering factors such as purpose, nature, amount, and effect on the market value of the original work. Thus, creators are encouraged to familiarize themselves with these concepts to minimize legal risks while maximizing creative expression. Another critical aspect of copyright understanding is recognizing the different types of content and their inherent protections. Original content crafted by creators automatically garners copyright protection, giving them exclusive rights to use, reproduce, and distribute their work. This means that creators can actively seek to monetize their original videos through advertising revenue, sponsorships, or merchandise without the fear of infringing on others rights. Conversely, the use of copyrighted music, clips from films, or other creators content requires explicit permission or licensing agreements. Content creators should also be aware of public domain works and Creative Commons licenses, which can provide avenues for legally incorporating existing content into their videos, thus fostering creativity while complying with legal norms.

Understanding copyright laws is not only about adhering to regulations but also about leveraging them to enhance creativity and engagement. Creators can effectively utilize their knowledge of copyright to build collaborative relationships with other creators, musicians, and brands, enabling opportunities for cross-promotion and reaching wider audiences. By respecting existing copyrights and seeking proper licenses for collaborations, creators can create unique and innovative content that appeals to viewers and stands out in a saturated market. Fostering a reputation for adhering to copyright laws can enhance a creators credibility within the community, potentially attracting brand partnerships and sponsorships. In this way, a thorough grasp of copyright not only protects creators but also serves as a catalyst for growth and connection in their YouTube ventures.

FAIR USE AND CONTENT CREATION

Navigating the intricacies of copyright law can be particularly daunting for content creators on platforms like YouTube, where the line between inspiration and infringement is often blurred. One concept that stands out in this context is fair use, a legal doctrine that allows limited use of copyrighted material without permission from the rights holder. This principle becomes especially pertinent for creators who seek to include existing works—whether they be music, video clips, or artwork—in their content. Fair use provides a framework under which creators can critique, comment, or even parody originals, offering not only legal protection but also a rich avenue for engaging storytelling. Understanding the four factors that determine fair use—purpose, nature, amount, and effect on the market—is crucial for creators striving to ensure their work remains compliant while still innovative and compelling. Cultivating a comprehensive understanding of fair use can significantly enhance a creator's ability to forge connections with their audience. Creators who adeptly utilize existing media can tap into shared cultural experiences that resonate with viewers, enhancing relatability and engagement. A creator utilizing clips from popular films or trending media can spark discussions and foster community, enriching the overall viewing experience. This approach requires a delicate balance; excessive reliance on third-party material or insufficient transformative elements can lead to copyright claims that undermine a channel's growth. Creators must not only focus on compliance but also harness fair use as an intentional strategy in crafting content that contributes to dialogue within the creative community, elevating their brand and channel successfully.

It is essential for content creators to remain vigilant and adapt their strategies as the landscape of fair use evolves, particularly in the digital age, marked by rapid technological advancements and changing societal norms. The fluidity of copyright interpretations means that what qualifies as fair use can shift, influenced by new case law and the unique interpretations of different jurisdictions. Creators should remain informed about updates to copyright legislation and may benefit from consulting legal experts to navigate complex scenarios. By proactively engaging with the nuances of fair use, creators can mitigate risks while fostering originality and innovation in their work. Those who master the principles of fair use not only safeguard their endeavors but also enrich the broader community by contributing diverse, transformative content that inspires dialogue and creativity.

PROTECTING YOUR CONTENT

Content creators must prioritize the formulation of a robust strategy to assert ownership over their work. This begins with understanding copyright laws and how they apply to various forms of media, including videos, music, and images. Establishing creative commons licenses or utilizing copyright notifications provides initial layers of protection against unauthorized usage. Having clear terms and conditions outlined on platforms like YouTube can significantly mitigate risks associated with intellectual property theft. By clearly marking content as original and delineating usage rights, creators can safeguard their intellectual efforts while maintaining control over their brand and message. This proactive approach not only deters potential infringement but also signals to viewers the value placed on original content within the YouTube community.

Equally important is the strategic use of digital tools that enhance content protection and foster audience engagement. Content ID, for instance, allows creators to track their uploaded works across the YouTube platform and either monetize or block unauthorized reproductions. Engaging with followers through social media can further serve as a means to build a community that respects original work. By cultivating a loyal audience, creators generate a support system that can help report instances of content theft and amplify their voice in the face of violation. Thus, the integration of technology with active audience participation not only ensures content remains protected but also nurtures a brand image that emphasizes authenticity and creator integrity. To truly capitalize on the protective measures in place, creators must also be vigilant and adaptable to evolving online landscapes. Regularly assessing the effectiveness of current strategies, staying updated with platform policy changes, and understanding emerging copyright laws can ensure that content remains secure over time. Creators should be prepared to err on the side of caution when navigating collaborations with other content producers, as partnerships can sometimes lead to disputes over ownership. Establishing clear agreements before undertaking joint projects can preemptively address potential conflicts, reinforcing the commitment to protecting one's intellectual property. By actively engaging with these protective measures, content creators can focus on what they do best—creating compelling content—with the confidence that their work is both visible and securely shielded from infringement.

Understanding copyright laws for YouTube creators

Pros	Cons
Legal protection	Risk of content strikes
Originality	Legal complexities
Monetization opportunities	Potential penalties
Viewer trust	Time-consuming
Creative collaboration	Need for licenses

XX. NETWORKING WITH OTHER CREATORS

Success on platforms like YouTube is often not a solitary endeavor; rather, it thrives on building relationships with other creators. Strategic networking allows individuals to tap into new audiences while sharing resources, knowledge, and skills. By forming alliances with creators who have complementary styles or niches, content producers can create collaborative projects that engage both parties audiences. This synergy not only boosts visibility but also fosters a sense of community among creators, which is pivotal in an industry that can often feel isolating. Whether through guest appearances, dual videos, or joint live streams, these collaborations can lead to exponential growth, as viewers are introduced to fresh perspectives and new content that keeps them coming back for more.

Engaging with other creators also facilitates invaluable feedback and support, which can be critical for growth and refinement. Constructive criticism from peers can provide insights that are difficult to glean in a vacuum, often identifying areas for improvement in content or presentation that a creator might overlook. Networking offers opportunities for mentorship, where experienced creators can guide newcomers through the labyrinthine paths of content creation, marketing, and brand building. This exchange of expertise not only enhances an individual's skillset but instills a sense of belonging within the broader creator community, helping to navigate the emotional rollercoaster often present in the pursuit of popular acclaim on platforms like YouTube. The impact of networking extends beyond mere viewership numbers; it lays the groundwork for sustainable success.

Creators who prioritize networking often find themselves positioned strategically within their niche, leading to collaborative ventures that generate fresh and engaging content. This interconnectedness can help mitigate the challenges posed by YouTubes frequently changing algorithms and policies, as a solid network can offer diversification and adaptability in approach. In a space that evolves rapidly, establishing a robust community of collaborators is not just beneficial; it is essential for creators aspiring to transition from obscurity to prominence in the ever-competitive landscape of YouTube.

BUILDING RELATIONSHIPS IN THE COMMUNITY

In a digital landscape where connections often feel superficial, establishing meaningful relationships within a community becomes paramount for YouTube creators. Engaging directly with viewers fosters a sense of ownership and loyalty, transforming a casual audience into a dedicated fan base. Creators can cultivate these relationships by responding to comments, conducting Q&A sessions, and involving subscribers in content decisions. This interactive approach not only personalizes the viewing experience but also prompts community members to feel valued and heard, which can lead to increased engagement metrics. As the channel develops an authentic community, creators can utilize the feedback gathered to refine their content, ensuring it resonates more profoundly with their audience's interests and preferences. Equally important in building relationships is the concept of collaboration. By partnering with other creators, individuals can tap into new audiences while simultaneously strengthening their community ties. Collaborative videos can introduce diverse perspectives and highlight shared values, making content more relatable and varied. These partnerships may involve joint projects, challenges, or interviews, and they not only expand reach but also enrich the content itself. Collaboration creates a network of mutual support, where creators and their communities can share resources and knowledge. This dynamic is crucial, particularly in the ever-evolving YouTube ecosystem, where relationships can influence exposure and success. Fostering a sense of community extends beyond mere viewer interaction; it encourages the creation of shared experiences and identities among subscribers. Organizing events, whether online or in-person, such as meet-and-greets, live streams, or themed gatherings, enhances interpersonal connections that transcend the digital divide. These encounters solidify the community ethos and provide opportunities for participants to engage face-to-face, thereby deepening their bond with the creator and each other. Initiatives like charitable campaigns or community-driven projects can uplift shared interests, promoting a culture of support and growth. When audience members unite under a common cause, they become more than just viewers; they evolve into advocates, effectively amplifying the creators reach and fostering an enduring sense of belonging.

ATTENDING CONFERENCES AND EVENTS

Engaging with industry conferences and events can significantly enhance a creators understanding of the dynamic landscape of YouTube. These gatherings provide invaluable opportunities for networking, where one can meet successful YouTubers, industry experts, and representatives from major brands. By participating in workshops and panel discussions, attendees gain insights into cutting-edge trends and best practices that are not always readily available online. This exchange of knowledge fosters not only personal growth but also the potential for collaborative opportunities. Such connections can lead to partnerships that amplify content reach and credibility, creating a ripple effect beneficial to a channels growth.

Conferences often showcase the latest tools and technologies that can transform the way creators produce and distribute content. Attendees can experience hands-on demonstrations of editing software, analytics tools, and marketing strategies that enhance a channel's visibility. Exposure to these innovations can inspire creators to incorporate new approaches to their work, making their content fresh and engaging to viewers. The practical advice obtained from industry leaders can streamline a creators approach to algorithm optimization and audience engagement. This can lead to more effective content strategies that resonate with viewers, fostering a loyal subscriber base.

The act of immersing oneself in a community of like-minded creators fuels motivation and creativity. The energy generated from shared experiences and challenges can reignite a passion for content creation that may have waned over time. Discussions with peers often reveal diverse perspectives and strategies that challenge one's own assumptions about the platform's best practices. Such interactions can spark innovative ideas that elevate a channels branding and messaging. Attending conferences and events becomes not merely an educational endeavor but a vital catalyst for sustained growth and reinvigoration in the competitive landscape of YouTube content creation.

COLLABORATIVE CONTENT CREATION

The process of creating content collaboratively often results in a broader range of ideas, perspectives, and creativity than one might achieve independently. By partnering with other content creators, individuals can pool their expertise, skills, and resources, leading to the development of multifaceted works that resonate more deeply with diverse audiences. Collaboration can manifest in various forms, from guest appearances and co-hosted series to joint projects that combine different styles and formats. This synergy not only enhances the quality of the content but also facilitates the cross-pollination of audiences, allowing each creator to engage with potentially new subscribers already vested in the opinions and personalities they trust. Collaborative content creation often encourages communities to rally around shared interests, fostering a sense of belonging that can enhance viewer loyalty and engagement.

Engaging with other creators also provides opportunities for learning and growth, a dynamic crucial for anyone navigating the competitive landscape of YouTube. Through collaboration, creators can acquire new skills and insights that expand their creative toolbox. Those who specialize in editing can benefit from working with storytellers, while performance artists may gain invaluable knowledge in technical production aspects. This, in turn, equips them to improve their own content and develop a more polished final product. The act of collaborating can lead to the formation of mentorships, as more experienced creators often share strategies and valuable insider knowledge that can expedite the growth trajectory for newcomers. The ripple effect of such exchanges can empower smaller channels to refine their voice, boost their contents visibility, and engage more authentically with their communities.

The advantageous outcomes of collaborative content creation hinge not merely on the act of working together but on the cultivation of authentic relationships within the creator community. Establishing trust and mutual respect with fellow content makers can lead to long-term partnerships that benefit all parties involved. Regular collaboration can create a feedback loop in which creators continuously inspire and motivate each other, resulting in enhanced innovative approaches to content development. These affiliations often lead to shared marketing efforts, where both creators actively promote each other's work, maximizing exposure and engagement. As the YouTube platform continues to evolve, those who adapt by integrating collaboration into their strategies will likely find themselves not only surviving but thriving amidst the complexities of algorithm changes and shifting viewer preferences. In this landscape, being part of a collaborative network can significantly elevate one's ability to attract and sustain a large and loyal subscriber base.

XXI. SCALING YOUR CHANNEL

In the modern landscape of digital content creation, leveraging social media platforms is paramount for any aspiring creator hoping to scale their YouTube channel. The interconnectedness of diverse platforms allows for a multi-faceted approach to audience engagement. Creators should utilize social media channels such as Instagram, Twitter, and TikTok to promote their YouTube videos, offering previews or behind-the-scenes content that creates anticipation. By cultivating a presence on these platforms, creators can provide additional value to their audience while also capturing the attention of potential subscribers. Engaging in timely conversations, utilizing trending hashtags, and collaborating with influencers can further enhance visibility. Social media acts as a powerful amplification tool that can convert casual viewers into dedicated subscribers, creating a solid foundation for sustained growth.

In conjunction with social media, consistency in content creation represents a critical factor in scaling a YouTube channel. Establishing a regular posting schedule not only fosters audience loyalty but also plays a significant role in how YouTube's algorithm promotes content. By delivering videos consistently, channels signal to their viewers and the platform that they are engaged and worthy of attention. Creators should target specific days and times for uploads, evaluating viewer engagement metrics to refine their approach. Consistency extends beyond timing; it also encompasses maintaining a coherent theme and style throughout the channel. By cultivating a recognizable brand identity, creators not only enhance their credibility but also build anticipation among their audience. The cumulative effect of these elements is an ever-expanding subscriber base, driven by viewers who return expectantly for new content.

Equally important in the journey to scaling a YouTube channel is the strategic use of data analytics to inform content decisions. YouTube provides a wealth of insights into viewer behavior, preferences, and engagement patterns, which can be invaluable for creators seeking to optimize their offerings. By analyzing metrics such as watch time, demographics, and click-through rates, creators can identify what resonates with their audience and what requires adjustment. This iterative process enables a creator to not only refine existing content but also craft future videos that align with viewers' interests. Experimenting with different content formats—such as live streams, tutorials, and collaborations—can yield insights into what captivates the audience most. By harnessing data effectively, creators can make informed strategic decisions that significantly bolster their ability to reach and retain subscribers, paving the way for a thriving channel.

STRATEGIES FOR GROWTH

An essential component of achieving growth on YouTube is creating content that resonates deeply with a target audience. Understanding the demographics and preferences of potential viewers allows creators to tailor their videos to meet those specific interests. Utilizing audience insights from YouTube analytics can inform decisions about video topics, formats, and styles. Engaging narratives that evoke emotions or provide value establish a connection, fostering a community around the channel. Incorporating trending themes while maintaining authenticity ensures that the content remains relatable yet innovative. Content creators should focus on delivering high-quality visuals and audio to enhance viewer experience, as first impressions are critical in retaining an audience. By investing time in researching relevant keywords and optimizing video titles, descriptions, and thumbnails, creators can improve discoverability, drawing viewers who are likely to subscribe for more engaging content.

Building a cohesive brand identity across various social media platforms significantly contributes to channel growth. Creating an online persona that reflects the channels niche bolsters authenticity and allows for stronger audience engagement. Consistently aligning content, aesthetics, and messaging with brand values creates recognition and loyalty among subscribers. Collaborating with other content creators can amplify visibility, allowing for cross-promotional opportunities that introduce the channel to new audiences. Leveraging social media channels to share behind-the-scenes content, teasers, and interactive posts fosters a sense of community and encourages viewer participation. Regularly engaging with viewers through comments and live sessions establishes a personal connection, inviting conversations that enhance viewer investment in the channel. A strong brand presence not only attracts new subscribers but also retains existing ones by continually fostering an engaged and dynamic community around the content creators mission.

Adapting to ongoing changes within YouTubes algorithm and audience preferences is crucial for sustained growth. The platform frequently updates its algorithm, which necessitates a flexible approach to content strategy. Creators must remain vigilant in monitoring industry trends and audience feedback to pivot their strategies effectively. Utilizing A/B testing—comparing different thumbnails, titles, or video formats—can provide valuable insights into viewer preferences and behaviors, enabling creators to refine their approach based on empirical data. Understanding the significance of video length, posting schedules, and viewer retention metrics is vital for optimizing content for visibility. Consistency not only pertains to upload frequency but also involves maintaining a quality standard that viewers can expect. By embracing new tools offered by the platform, such as shorts or live-streaming features, creators can diversify their content types, keeping the channel fresh and inviting, which, in turn, lays the groundwork for exponential growth.

EXPANDING CONTENT OFFERINGS

In a landscape as dynamic as YouTube, adaptability plays a crucial role in content creation. As trends evolve and audience preferences shift, content creators must continually reassess their offerings to maintain relevance. Diversifying video formats—such as incorporating live streams, vlogs, tutorials, and interviews—can cater to a broader audience while refreshing the channel's creative approach. Experimenting with series-based content cultivates viewer investment, encouraging them to return for subsequent installments. This not only boosts engagement but also creates opportunities for deeper connections with the audience, fostering a loyal viewer base. By championing varied content types, creators can efficiently respond to analytics and feedback, ensuring they remain aligned with viewer expectations and interests.

Engaging with audiences beyond the confines of traditional videos enhances the connection and fosters community. Integrating interactive elements, such as Q&A sessions or polls on social media platforms, can facilitate two-way communication, allowing viewers to feel more involved in the content-making process. Such engagement can serve as a vital resource for identifying new content angles and potential topics of interest. Creators might consider submitting ideas for collaborative projects, allowing for cross-pollination of audiences and shared experiences. As creators expand their reach through collaboration, they simultaneously enrich their content library and appeal to diverse viewer demographics, further enhancing their growth potential. This approach exemplifies the power of community-building in facilitating a more robust content offering.

The expansion of content offerings is not merely about quantity but quality driven by audience understanding. Employing data analytics tools can reveal viewer behavior and preferences, providing insights that inform the direction of new content endeavors. It is essential for content creators to monitor engagement metrics, such as watch time, likes, and comments, to identify what resonates most effectively. By tailoring content to meet these metrics while remaining authentic to their personal brand, creators not only bolster their credibility but can also innovate within their niches. A strategic, data-informed approach enables more effective outreach while paving the way for sustained growth and enhanced subscriber loyalty. This multifaceted strategy underscores the importance of evolving content offerings as a fundamental step for aspiring YouTube creators aiming for long-term success.

DIVERSIFYING PLATFORMS

In an increasingly competitive digital landscape, the importance of diversifying platforms cannot be overstated. Building a significant presence solely on YouTube may appear appealing, but relying on a single channel poses substantial risks. Algorithm changes and shifts in user preferences can dramatically impact visibility and engagement. By extending reach to various social media platforms such as Instagram, TikTok, and Twitter, creators can enhance their visibility and attract different segments of their audience. Each platform offers unique tools and features that can be leveraged to create tailored content, thereby increasing overall engagement and awareness. Utilizing multiple channels fosters cross-promotion opportunities, allowing creators to channel viewers from one platform to another, thus bolstering subscriber growth and overall brand cohesiveness.

Beyond risk mitigation, platform diversification also enables creators to experiment with varying content styles and engagement strategies. Different platforms cater to different content forms—short, punchy videos thrive on TikTok, while Instagram is excellent for visually striking imagery and stories. This variety invites innovation, pushing creators to adapt their message and artistic expression to fit each platforms character and audience. Testing content across several outlets aids in discovering what resonates most with viewers; this knowledge can significantly enhance a creator's main YouTube offerings. By understanding their audiences preferences across platforms, creators can refine their content strategy, ensuring that they meet viewer expectations and maintain engagement over time.

Engaging with multiple platforms can foster a more holistic relationship with audiences. Each social media channel provides unique ways to interact with viewers, from comments and direct messages to live streams and polls. This enriched interaction fosters community-building and deepens viewer loyalty, which is crucial for sustainable growth. As creators cultivate followings across platforms, they not only draw in larger audiences but also parachute into new opportunities for collaboration and sponsorships that may not have been available on a single channel. This interconnectedness also enhances analytics capabilities, granting creators insights into how their audience interacts with diverse content types. By embracing diversification, creators position themselves for long-term success, adaptability, and expansive growth, which are essential in the fast-evolving digital arena.

XXII. CASE STUDIES OF SUCCESSFUL CREATORS

In the landscape of YouTube, certain creators have explored innovative strategies that not only increased their subscriber counts but also solidified their presence in niche markets. One compelling case is that of Jenna Marbles, whose authenticity and relatable content resonated with millions. Starting her channel in 2006 with humorous pet videos and personal vlogs, she quickly established a brand characterized by genuine engagement with her audience. She harnessed the power of storytelling and humor to create a community around her content. Jenna's ability to adapt her style and subjects over time, while remaining true to her original voice, ultimately contributed to her status as one of YouTubes earliest success stories. This adaptability in her content not only attracted a diverse audience but also kept her loyal viewers engaged, demonstrating how a creator can evolve while maintaining the essence of their brand. Another exemplary case is Marques Brownlee, known as MKBHD, whose focus on technology reviews and insightful commentary has garnered him a significant following. By emphasizing quality over quantity, Marques invested in high production values for his videos, showcasing a keen understanding of how presentation impacts viewer perception. His in-depth analyses and professional approach not only educated his audience on complex tech products but also established him as a credible authority in the field. His skillful use of social media amplified his reach and visibility, as clips of his reviews would often spark conversations across various platforms. Brownlee exemplifies how a creator can leverage expertise and aesthetics to build a distinct niche on YouTube while simultaneously diversifying content types, setting an example for aspiring creators seeking to carve out their own paths in the competitive ecosystem.

In yet another vein, the culinary creator Binging with Babish exemplifies how unique branding can lead to exceptional success. By combining cooking demonstrations with elements of popular media, Andrew Rea creatively engages his audience through the preparation of dishes inspired by films and television shows. His strategic approach to content—pairing culinary skills with nostalgic references—has not only captivated food enthusiasts but also attracted a broader audience with diverse interests. Through clear narratives and visually stunning presentations, Rea effectively transforms simple cooking tutorials into captivating entertainment. His case illustrates that understanding ones audience and integrating elements of their interests into the content can significantly enhance engagement and subscriber growth. By successfully merging culinary art with popular culture, Binging with Babish serves as a testament to the potential of niche creativity in building a widely resonant brand on YouTube.

ANALYZING TOP YOUTUBERS

The success of leading YouTubers can often be attributed to their adept understanding of audience engagement and content strategy. These creators meticulously assess viewer preferences, responding to trends and feedback to fine-tune their offerings for optimal impact. Top YouTubers frequently analyze their analytics for patterns in viewer retention and engagement, thereby identifying the types of content that resonate best with their audiences. They engage actively with their followers through comments and social media, fostering a sense of community that encourages loyalty and repeat viewership. This two-way interaction not only keeps their audience invested but also provides invaluable insights for future content. Over time, successful creators build a unique brand identity that reflects their personality and values, making their channels distinctive and relatable. This blend of strategic assessment and authentic connection underpins the solid foundation of their expansive subscriber bases. The utilization of YouTube's algorithm is another critical factor that plays a pivotal role in the success of popular creators. By understanding how the platform prioritizes content, successful YouTubers craft videos that align with algorithmic preferences, which often favor engaging, high-quality, and relevant material. They strategically select keywords, create compelling thumbnails, and structure their content to enhance discoverability. Implementing tactics like optimizing video titles and tags can significantly boost a creator's visibility in searches, leading to higher engagement rates. Popular creators often maintain consistency in posting schedules, a strategy that not only helps with algorithmic favorability but also establishes a reliable rhythm that keeps viewers returning for more. This deliberate alignment with YouTube's mechanics underscores the necessity of technical acumen in navigating the platform, illustrating how creators can harness these tools to significantly expand their reach. Diversification of content and income streams is a hallmark of successful YouTubers, allowing them to maintain relevance and financial stability in an ever-changing landscape. Many of these creators venture beyond traditional video content by exploring various formats such as vlogs, tutorials, collaborations, or live streams, capturing the diverse interests of their audiences. This adaptability not only helps maintain viewer interest but also positions them to capitalize on emerging trends and niches. With the rise of brand partnerships and sponsorships, influencers have realized the importance of professional networking, leveraging their platforms for monetization opportunities. This business-savvy approach often includes launching merchandise, offering exclusive content through subscription models, or establishing affiliate marketing links. By creating multiple revenue streams, these creators ensure sustained growth while enhancing their brand equity, further solidifying their prominence in the competitive realm of YouTube.

LESSONS LEARNED FROM THEIR JOURNEYS

The pathways to success on YouTube illuminate the essential role of adaptability in a rapidly evolving digital landscape. Many creators discover that the strategies that worked last year may not yield the same results today. As algorithms change and audience preferences shift, it becomes imperative for content producers to remain agile, continually testing new ideas and formats. This journey has taught many that flexibility is not merely a survival tactic; it is a catalyst for innovation. Successful YouTubers often emphasize the importance of feedback loops, where they actively seek viewer input to refine their content. By noting which videos perform well and why, content creators can pivot with purpose, transforming negative trends into positive growth opportunities. Thus, the ability to embrace change and evolve accordingly is a crucial lesson learned from navigating the complexities of the YouTube platform. Equally significant in the journey to subscriber growth is the cultivation of a genuine community around ones content. Many prominent YouTubers highlight the importance of interaction with their audience, which fosters a sense of belonging and loyalty. By engaging viewers through comments, live chats, and social media platforms, creators can humanize their brand and build lasting connections. This relationship not only boosts engagement metrics but often translates into higher viewer retention and an expanded reach. Successful content creators recognize that transparency about their own journeys—sharing both struggles and triumphs—resonates deeply with audiences. Through authenticity, they invite viewers into their world, creating a narrative that encourages them to invest emotionally in the channel. Thus, the lesson of community building underscores the relational aspect of content creation, demonstrating that true success is rooted in the connections formed with others. Mastering the technical aspects of content creation emerges as a fundamental lesson gleaned from the journeys of successful YouTubers. From understanding video editing software to optimizing thumbnails and titles, creators quickly learn that the visual presentation of their content plays a pivotal role in attracting viewers. Many find that investing time in learning these technical skills not only enhances the quality of their work but also boosts their confidence in producing content that stands out amidst a sea of competition. Data analytics become a powerful ally in this process; by analyzing view counts, audience demographics, and watch times, creators can glean critical insights that drive future content strategies. This skillful blend of creativity and analytics empowers YouTubers to craft videos that not only draw in viewers but also sustain their interest. Emphasizing technical proficiency, therefore, illustrates a crucial dimension of the YouTube journey, asserting its importance in achieving lasting success.

APPLYING SUCCESS STRATEGIES

Creating impactful content is often cited as the cornerstone of success on any platform, and YouTube is no exception. Engaging content that connects with viewers not only holds their attention but also prompts them to subscribe and share. To achieve this, creators should focus on understanding their target audience, identifying what resonates with them, and tailoring content accordingly. Implementing storytelling techniques enhances emotional connections, making viewers more likely to invest in a creators journey. Beyond just storytelling, it is imperative to consistently evaluate feedback and analytics to adapt and refine content strategies. This willingness to pivot based on audience engagement ensures that the channel remains relevant and continues to attract new subscribers, thus amplifying the chances for success. Channel optimization is a technical yet vital strategy that often determines a creator's visibility on YouTube. Keywords play a crucial role in helping the platforms algorithm assess content relevance, so creators should employ comprehensive keyword research to enhance video discoverability. This entails crafting compelling titles, descriptions, and tags that align with trending search terms related to their niche. Understanding and utilizing playlists can keep viewers on channels longer, as they provide an organized way for users to consume related content. High-quality thumbnails that stand out in the crowded YouTube landscape are equally important, as they significantly influence click-through rates. By mastering these optimization tools, creators can ensure their content reaches a wider audience, ultimately facilitating channel growth.

Embracing a multifaceted approach to promotional strategies can substantially enhance a creators reach. Utilizing platforms like Instagram, Twitter, and TikTok enables creators to connect with different segments of their audience and drive traffic back to their YouTube channel. Cross-promotion with other creators can also be beneficial, as it encourages subscribers to explore and engage with new content. Consistency is key; maintaining a regular upload schedule fosters anticipation among viewers and establishes a reliable rhythm for content consumption. Importantly, staying adaptable and informed about ongoing trends and shifts in the YouTube ecosystem prepares creators to navigate changes effectively. By integrating these diverse strategies, the path to cultivating a substantial subscriber base becomes not only achievable but also sustainable.

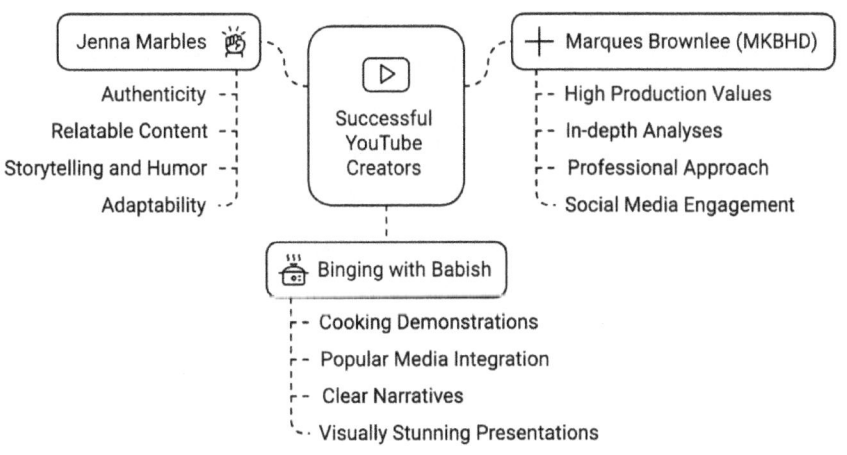

XXIII. THE FUTURE OF YOUTUBE

As the landscape of digital media continues to evolve, YouTube is poised to implement innovative features that could further enhance viewer engagement and creator visibility. One area that shows promise is the integration of augmented reality (AR) and virtual reality (VR) into video content. By allowing viewers to immerse themselves in a 360-degree experience, creators can develop more captivating narratives and interactive experiences. Such advancements could democratize content creation, enabling a broader range of storytellers to share unique perspectives, while also providing audiences with more dynamic ways to interact with their favorite creators. Advancements in AI technology may facilitate improved content recommendations, leading to more personalized viewing experiences and higher levels of audience retention. In this way, YouTube can maintain its relevance in an era marked by rapid technological change. The platform's ongoing commitment to diversity and inclusivity will also play a crucial role in shaping its future. As society grapples with issues related to representation, YouTube has an opportunity to become a leader in promoting voices from underrepresented communities. By prioritizing equitable content distribution and providing creators from diverse backgrounds with tools and resources, the platform can broaden the spectrum of narratives that are shared. This commitment is not only beneficial for creators but also enriches the viewing experience for audiences who seek authentic stories that resonate with their own experiences. YouTubes algorithms could be adjusted to highlight a wider variety of content, effectively disrupting the traditional influencer hierarchy that often prioritizes mainstream creators. In doing so, the platform could foster a richer tapestry of content that reflects the global community more fully.

Looking ahead, the monetization landscape of YouTube is likely to undergo further transformation, which could present both opportunities and challenges for creators. As advertisers seek to connect with niche audiences, models of sponsorship and brand partnerships may evolve, encouraging creators to diversify their revenue streams beyond traditional ad placements. Platforms for direct viewer support, such as memberships and merchandise sales, will likely gain popularity, allowing creators to cultivate deeper relationships with their audience. This shift may also intensify competition among creators, requiring them to innovate continuously and refine their personal brands to stand out in an increasingly crowded space. Balancing the need for artistic integrity with market demands could become a pivotal challenge as content creators navigate these changes, ultimately influencing the trajectory of their channels and the YouTube ecosystem as a whole.

EMERGING TRENDS IN CONTENT CREATION

The landscape of content creation is shifting rapidly, with new technologies and platforms continually reshaping the way creators engage with their audiences. One significant trend is the rise of immersive content, particularly through virtual reality (VR) and augmented reality (AR). These technologies provide a unique opportunity for creators to deliver experiences that transcend traditional video formats, immersing viewers in interactive environments. As the hardware becomes more accessible, content creators are increasingly exploring ways to integrate AR and VR into their storytelling, enhancing viewer engagement and creating memorable experiences. This innovation not only broadens the scope of content available but also challenges creators to think outside conventional methods, paving the way for a new era where audiences can actively participate in the narratives presented. Another prominent trend transforming content creation is the growing influence of live streaming. Platforms like YouTube, Twitch, and Instagram have popularized the concept of real-time engagement, allowing creators to interact with their audiences instantaneously. This immediacy fosters a sense of community and authenticity, as viewers can witness the unfiltered personality of the creator and participate in discussions, polls, and Q&A sessions. The impact of live streaming extends beyond mere entertainment; it enables creators to cultivate a loyal fan base and develop deeper connections with their audience. As algorithms increasingly favor content that encourages viewer interaction, embracing live formats can significantly enhance a channel's visibility and growth trajectory in the competitive YouTube ecosystem. Continuous adaptation is essential for sustained success in content creation, particularly as audience preferences evolve. The integration of data analytics into content strategy has emerged as a crucial trend, allowing creators to make informed decisions based on viewer behavior and engagement metrics. This analytical approach enables content creators to identify what resonates most with their audience, optimize video formats, and refine their branding strategy. Understanding audience demographics and viewing habits can aid creators in tailoring their content to fit niche markets. As competition intensifies on platforms like YouTube, those who effectively leverage analytics to inform their creative direction are more likely to stand out, ensuring their content remains relevant and compelling in an ever-changing digital landscape.

PREDICTIONS FOR THE PLATFORM

As the digital landscape evolves, we can expect significant shifts in how platforms like YouTube operate, particularly in terms of content curation and user engagement. In the near future, algorithms are likely to incorporate more advanced artificial intelligence capabilities that better understand audience preferences and viewing habits. This could lead to a hyper-personalized experience, where viewers are served content that aligns almost perfectly with their interests, pushing creators to understand audience analytics more deeply than ever before. Such advancements will likely reward those who adapt quickly to the changing technological environment, as the ability to produce content that resonates with specific viewer segments becomes increasingly crucial. Emerging trends suggest that video formats will diversify significantly, integrating more interactive elements to keep audiences engaged. We may see a rise in live streaming and augmented reality experiences, allowing for a more immersive viewer interaction. Short-form content is gaining traction as platforms increasingly prioritize bite-sized videos that can capture attention rapidly. This evolution necessitates that content creators refine their strategies, experimenting with different formats to discover what resonates most with their audience. In doing so, they must strike a balance between maintaining their authentic voice and adapting to new trends that attract viewers in a crowded marketplace. Understanding monetization will continue to be a vital consideration for creators looking to transition from hobbyists to professional content producers. As competition intensifies and alternative platforms emerge, YouTube may adjust its monetization policies, prompting creators to diversify their income streams. This could include improved integration with merchandise, subscription models, and sponsorships, all of which require a keen understanding of not only audience engagement but also brand alignment. Those who master these novel monetization strategies while fostering community engagement are more likely to thrive amidst the evolving landscape of digital content creation, ensuring not just survival but success in the competitive YouTube ecosystem.

ADAPTING TO FUTURE CHANGES

Navigating the shifting landscape of digital content requires a keen awareness of emerging trends and technological advancements. For aspiring YouTube creators, adaptation is not merely beneficial; it is essential for survival in an extremely competitive environment. As algorithms evolve, platform policies change, and viewer preferences shift, those who refuse to alter their strategies risk obsolescence. Building an agile mindset allows creators to experiment with formats, topics, and technologies, whether that involves exploring emerging genres like live-streaming or incorporating new editing techniques. This dynamic approach not only enhances content quality but also cultivates resilience against unforeseen challenges, laying a foundation for sustained growth and engagement.

Leveraging data analytics serves as a pivotal strategy for gauging viewer response and fine-tuning content. By examining metrics such as watch time, engagement rates, and demographic information, creators can make informed decisions about their content direction. This analytical approach fosters a deeper understanding of audience preferences, which can guide not only video creation but also marketing strategies. Creators should regularly assess their performance and be willing to pivot based on these insights, whether that means adjusting video length, experimenting with different thumbnails, or collaborating with other creators to tap into new audiences. Such adaptability ensures that content resonates with viewers, forging a stronger connection and fostering loyalty over time.

In an arena where perseverance is crucial, maintaining a growth-oriented mindset empowers creators to embrace change rather than fear it. The path to success on YouTube is marked by continuous learning and evolution; static strategies are unlikely to yield long-term results. Engaging with the community, soliciting feedback, and observing competitors can spark innovative ideas that set a creator apart. As the platform itself evolves, so must the creators within it. Embracing challenges not only reinforces a channels relevance but also inspires confidence among viewers who seek fresh and engaging content. Adaptability transforms potential setbacks into opportunities for reinvention, ensuring that creators not only survive but thrive in an ever-changing digital landscape.

XXIV. COMMON MISTAKES TO AVOID

Navigating the complexities of YouTube can be a daunting task, particularly for newcomers who may be unaccustomed to the platforms intricacies. One common mistake that aspiring creators often make is underestimating the importance of audience engagement. Failing to actively interact with viewers through comments, polls, and community posts can lead to disconnection, diminishing the emotional investment audiences have in a channel. Successful YouTubers understand that fostering a sense of community is critical; responding to comments and requesting feedback can turn casual viewers into devoted fans. This approach not only enhances viewer loyalty but also encourages higher retention rates, which positively impacts video performance metrics. Engaging with the audience builds a dialogue that fuels growth and keeps the creator informed about what resonates most with their viewers.

Another significant pitfall involves neglecting the power of consistent branding. An inconsistent aesthetic—ranging from thumbnail designs to video formats—can confuse potential subscribers and dilute the creators message. Establishing a clear, recognizable brand identity across all content is essential in making a memorable impression. This means adhering to a coherent color scheme, visual style, and tone of voice in every video release. Creators should optimize their video titles and descriptions to effectively convey their brand. This level of consistency reinforces the creator's presence in the crowded space of YouTube, ensuring that current and potential subscribers can easily identify their content. A well-defined brand not only aids in audience retention but also makes it easier to implement strategies for collaboration and monetization, ultimately setting the stage for long-term success.

Neglecting the importance of analytics can severely hinder growth on the platform. Many creators make the mistake of disregarding YouTube's vast array of data insights available in the Creator Studio. Failing to analyze key metrics such as watch time, audience retention, and click-through rates can lead to missed opportunities for optimization and content refinement. By studying these analytics, creators can identify which videos are performing well and why, allowing them to replicate successful strategies moving forward. This data-driven approach informs decisions about when to post, how to tailor content to specific audience interests, and what kinds of promotions may be effective. In a competitive landscape where viewer preferences can shift rapidly, being adaptable and responsive to analytics can be the difference between stagnation and explosive growth on a channel.

PITFALLS IN CONTENT CREATION

Navigating the landscape of content creation often reveals various pitfalls that can hinder a creators progress toward success on platforms like YouTube. One primary challenge is the overwhelming pressure to produce content consistently, which can lead to burnout and diminished creative quality. Creators often feel compelled to upload videos at a breakneck pace, fearing that any lapse will result in lost engagement. Unfortunately, this mindset may sacrifice originality and passion—two critical components of compelling content. When creators prioritize quantity over quality, audiences can quickly lose interest, leading to stagnation in growth. Thus, striking a balance between maintaining a steady upload schedule while ensuring that each piece of content is meaningful becomes a vital lesson for burgeoning YouTubers. Equally significant is the common misstep of ignoring audience feedback and analytics. Many creators begin their journey with a personal vision of what they believe is appealing, sometimes overlooking the specific preferences of their target demographic. Understanding audience engagement metrics, such as watch time and viewer retention, offers invaluable insights into what resonates with viewers. When creators neglect this aspect, they risk alienating their audience and producing content that fails to meet their interests. Leveraging feedback—not just within comments, but also through social media interactions and analytics—empowers creators to refine their approach and deliver what their audience desires. This responsiveness not only builds a loyal community but also enhances the likelihood of organic growth.

Moving forward, creators must also be vigilant about the evolving nature of social media algorithms. YouTubes algorithm is known for its intricacies and frequent updates, which can drastically affect video visibility. Relying too heavily on a singular strategy can become a pitfall if trends change or if a creator's approach no longer aligns with platform dynamics. Staying informed about algorithmic changes and experimenting with diverse content types can mitigate this risk. Fostering adaptability allows creators to pivot in response to shifts in viewer interests and external trends, thereby maintaining relevance. Embracing flexibility not only aids in sustaining viewer engagement but also fortifies a creator's resilience against the inevitable vicissitudes of the digital media landscape.

MISTAKES IN MARKETING STRATEGIES

In the competitive landscape of YouTube, one misstep can significantly undermine the effectiveness of a marketing strategy. A common error involves neglecting to define a clear target audience, leading creators to produce content that lacks focus and fails to engage viewers meaningfully. Without a well-researched target demographic, it becomes difficult to tailor content that resonates with the intended audience, ultimately resulting in low viewer retention rates and minimal subscriber growth. This oversight often leads to inconsistent branding, where the channels overall image becomes diluted and confusing. Successful creators understand that a precise target audience not only shapes their content but also influences their engagement methods and promotional activities, thus bolstering their ability to connect authentically with viewers.

Another critical mistake arises from the disregard for data analytics, which offers priceless insights into audience behavior and content performance. Many novice creators may overlook this tool, instead relying solely on intuition or personal preferences when deciding what to produce next. Ignoring analytics can lead to repeated failures, as content that doesn't align with audience interests or viewing habits may fail to gain traction. Creators who do not actively monitor the results of their marketing efforts miss opportunities for improvement and optimization. By analyzing which videos perform well and understanding audience demographics, successful YouTubers can pivot their strategy in real-time, ensuring their content remains relevant and appealing. This data-driven approach empowers creators to experiment confidently, engage in effective targeted marketing, and refine their strategies for sustained growth.

Adaptability remains paramount in an ever-evolving platform like YouTube. Sticking to rigid plans or outdated strategies can prove detrimental as algorithm changes and audience preferences shift. Creators who fail to remain flexible may find their once-successful formulas increasingly ineffective. A marketing strategy that was successful in one year may not yield the same results in a different context, especially as new trends emerge and user engagement patterns fluctuate. Thus, successful YouTubers continuously evaluate their content and marketing approaches, adjusting them to reflect current standards and expectations. This willingness to evolve not only enhances the relevance of their channels but also instills a sense of authenticity that viewers appreciate, cultivating a loyal audience base that is crucial for long-term success.

AVOIDING BURNOUT

Creating a successful YouTube channel can be an exhilarating journey, but it is equally important to recognize the potential pitfalls along the way, particularly the risk of burnout. As content creators often push themselves to meet demanding schedules and maintain engagement, the pressure can lead to emotional and physical exhaustion. Acknowledging the signs of burnout—such as fatigue, decreased motivation, and irritability—empowers creators to implement preventive measures. Building a sustainable content plan that prioritizes quality over quantity allows creators to produce authentic and engaging material without succumbing to the frenetic pace often seen in the digital landscape.

Time management plays a pivotal role in avoiding the overwhelming stress associated with content creation. Setting realistic schedules and boundaries is essential, ensuring that creators allocate time not only for video production but also for relaxation and personal activities. Incorporating breaks and off days into ones routine cultivates a balanced lifestyle, ultimately enhancing creativity and productivity. Engaging with fellow creators and fostering a supportive community can also alleviate feelings of isolation, as shared experiences and encouragement can serve as vital support systems during challenging periods.

Maintaining a passion for the craft serves as a powerful antidote to burnout. Creators should continually seek inspiration, whether through new ideas, collaborations, or by revisiting the fundamental reasons that sparked their initial drive to become content creators. Emphasizing personal growth and exploration allows creators to innovate without the relentless burden of expectation. When the joy of creation is prioritized over metrics and algorithms, the likelihood of burnout diminishes significantly, paving the way for sustained success and authenticity in the ever-changing ecosystem of YouTube.

XXV. RESOURCES FOR YOUTUBE CREATORS

Navigating the vast landscape of YouTube requires a wealth of resources to develop a strong channel and engage with a growing audience. Among the most valuable tools available to creators are video editing software and graphic design applications. Programs such as Adobe Premiere Pro and Final Cut Pro offer advanced editing capabilities, enabling creators to produce high-quality content that is visually appealing and professional. Platforms like Canva and Adobe Spark facilitate the creation of eye-catching thumbnails and channel art, which are critical for attracting potential subscribers. These resources not only enhance the aesthetic quality of videos but also help to establish a cohesive brand identity, ultimately contributing to the creators visibility and credibility within a saturated market.

Data analytics play a central role in honing content strategy. Utilizing YouTube Analytics allows creators to scrutinize viewer engagement, demographics, and traffic sources—insights that can shape future content decisions. Creators should monitor metrics such as watch time, click-through rates, and audience retention to identify what resonates with their audience. Supplementing this with tools like TubeBuddy or VidIQ can unveil even deeper insights into keywords and trends, guiding creators to optimize video titles, tags, and descriptions accordingly. By leveraging these analytics and optimization tools, creators can not only refine their current content but also strategically plan future uploads that align with viewer preferences, increasing the likelihood of attracting new subscribers and maintaining viewer loyalty.

The importance of community engagement cannot be overstated. Tools such as social media platforms, Discord servers, and creator forums can foster interaction between creators and their audiences, enhancing the viewer experience. Engaging with comments, conducting polls, and hosting live Q&A sessions not only humanizes the creator but also cultivates a loyal fan base that feels valued and invested in the channel. Collaborations with other creators can amplify reach and provide fresh perspectives, driving both channels growth. Resources for community building are essential for creating a nurturing space that promotes discussion and fosters a sense of belonging among viewers, thus serving as a foundation for sustained success on YouTube.

ONLINE COURSES AND TUTORIALS

In today's digital age, the proliferation of online courses and tutorials serves as a powerful catalyst for aspiring YouTubers seeking to hone their skills. These resources can be invaluable for anyone looking to navigate the complexities of video production, content strategy, and audience engagement. Platforms such as Coursera, Udemy, and even YouTube itself offer structured learning experiences that cover everything from basic filming techniques to advanced video editing software. Participants can cultivate a diverse skill set, often under the guidance of industry experts, which helps them not only in the technical aspects of video creation but also in understanding market demands and viewer preferences. This comprehensive approach equips creators with the necessary tools to produce high-quality content, fostering growth in a competitive landscape.

Engagement with online tutorials and courses allows content

creators to discover various educational methodologies, enhancing their adaptability on YouTube. Learning about SEO practices specifically tailored for video content can significantly improve a creator's visibility on the platform. Many online learning platforms provide insights into algorithm dynamics, which are crucial for strategically positioning videos to reach broader audiences. Creators can participate in community forums and collaborative projects that foster peer support and feedback. This interactive aspect enhances the learning experience, imparting a sense of accountability and camaraderie that can be pivotal in maintaining motivation throughout one's growth journey. The integration of online tutorials and courses into a YouTube creator's toolkit is vital for sustained success. With a foundation built on continuous learning and skill refinement, individuals can stay attuned to the ever-evolving trends within the platform. These educational resources empower creators to innovate and diversify their content, creating unique value propositions that resonate with diverse audience segments. By leveraging acquired knowledge from these courses, aspiring content creators can strategically cultivate their channels, leading to increased subscriber retention and engagement. This dedication to learning not only positions creators for immediate success but also ensures they remain adaptable through the many shifts in the digital landscape, allowing them to thrive long-term.

BOOKS AND GUIDES

In an era dominated by digital media, comprehensive resources on YouTube growth can serve as invaluable tools for aspiring content creators. Guides and books dedicated to mastering the platform often distill the experiences of seasoned YouTubers, presenting strategies that have proven successful in the competitive landscape of online content. Whether focusing on creating engaging thumbnails to optimize click-through rates or emphasizing the importance of storytelling within videos, these resources help demystify the complexities of audience engagement. By analyzing case studies of channels that have achieved exponential growth, creators glean insights into market trends and viewer psychology, providing them with a foundation to craft their own user-centric content. Armed with this knowledge, new creators can embark on their journey with more confidence and a clearer roadmap.

The role of analytical tools cannot be overstated when it comes to refining video content and understanding audience dynamics. Many books on YouTube success emphasize the significance of data analytics, enabling creators to make informed decisions about their content strategy. By closely examining viewer demographics, watch time, and engagement metrics, creators can identify what resonates with their audience and adjust their approach accordingly. This process of continuous improvement not only aids in content creation but also highlights the necessity of adaptability in a rapidly changing digital environment. Over time, these insights empower creators to evolve their strategies and maintain relevance, with analytics serving as both a guiding framework and a measuring stick for growth. As such, incorporating analytical insights can transform an intuitive approach into a methodical strategy that supports sustained subscriber growth. Crafting a personal brand is another crucial aspect explored in guides focusing on YouTube excellence. Many resources highlight the interplay between authenticity and branding, encouraging creators to showcase their unique personalities and expertise. This distinctive voice fosters a deeper connection with the audience, making the content more relatable and engaging. A creator who authentically shares their journey, complete with challenges and triumphs, fosters loyalty among viewers who appreciate transparency. Establishing a strong brand image can facilitate cross-platform synergies, enabling creators to extend their reach beyond YouTube, utilizing social media and other channels as promotional extensions. In a landscape where viewers often seek connections over mere entertainment, a well-defined personal brand can be the differentiating factor that transforms casual viewers into dedicated subscribers, ultimately guiding creators towards the achievement of their goals.

COMMUNITY SUPPORT GROUPS

Engagement with community support groups serves as a significant catalyst for aspiring YouTube creators seeking to make their mark on the platform. These groups often provide mentorship and a sense of belonging that can greatly enhance a creators confidence and skill development. In many instances, newcomers can share their struggles and triumphs with like-minded individuals who understand the unique challenges of content creation. Beyond emotional support, these groups facilitate the exchange of practical advice, from content optimization techniques to insights on navigating YouTube's ever-evolving algorithms. Such collaborative environments foster creativity and innovation, empowering creators to adapt and refine their strategies in real-time while gaining inspiration from the collective experiences of their peers.

The power of community support groups extends beyond mere moral encouragement; they can also serve as effective platforms for networking and collaboration. Forming connections with others in the group can open doors to potential partnerships, where creators can co-produce content or cross-promote each other's channels. This is particularly advantageous for those just starting, as collaborations can exponentially increase visibility and subscriber numbers. A creator with a small but engaged audience can benefit from the exposure provided by a more established partner, while the latter can tap into fresh ideas and creativity. These connections can lead to learning opportunities through workshops or discussions, helping members stay informed about industry trends and best practices that can further their growth. The integration of community support groups into ones YouTube journey not only fosters personal growth but also creates a robust network that enhances long-term success. By leveraging the collective knowledge and resources of fellow creators, individuals can navigate the complexities of content creation with greater ease and efficacy. The shared experiences within these groups can illuminate various paths to excellence, illustrating that success is often not achieved in isolation but through the synergy created by engagement and collaboration. For those committed to scaling their channels, the insights and encouragement gained from such communities can be invaluable, propelling them closer to their goal of reaching millions of subscribers and establishing a resilient presence on YouTube.

Essential Resources for YouTube Creators

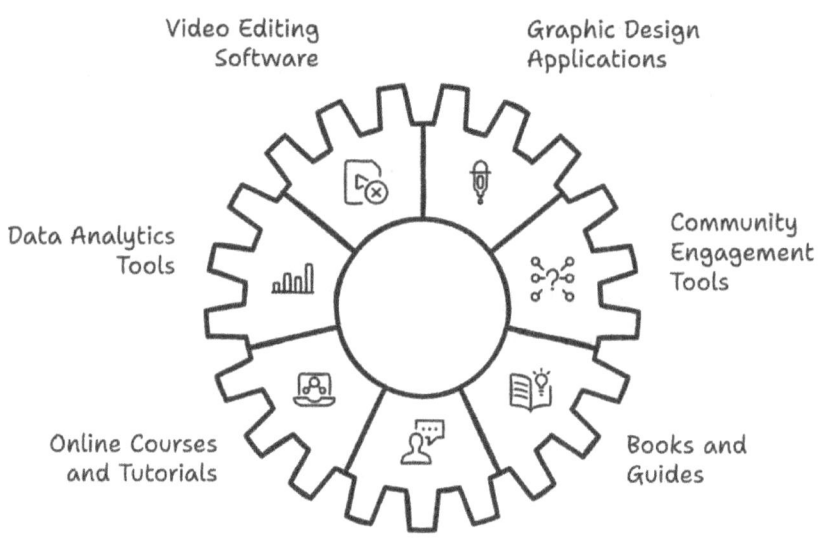

XXVI. CONCLUSION

The culmination of this comprehensive guide rests on the understanding that success on YouTube is neither random nor purely reliant on luck; instead, it is the result of strategic planning and execution. Throughout the journey, we have explored the multifaceted approaches that successful creators employ to attract and retain millions of subscribers. From establishing a distinctive brand identity to cultivating authenticity in content delivery, each element plays a critical role in fostering audience loyalty. By adopting a methodical strategy that incorporates thorough audience research and tailoring content to meet their preferences, creators can not only enhance visibility but also solidify their connection with viewers.

The evolving landscape of YouTube necessitates a commitment to continuous learning and adaptation. As trends emerge and algorithms change, staying informed is essential for any creator wishing to maintain relevance in a competitive environment. The practical advice laid out in this essay regarding data analytics, video optimization, and marketing strategies serves as both a roadmap and a toolkit for navigating these shifts. Emphasizing engagement and consistency, along with a responsive approach to audience feedback, empowers creators to refine their methods and stays relevant amid changing viewer expectations.

The pathway from obscurity to prominence on YouTube is marked by perseverance, adaptability, and an unwavering focus on one's audience. Individuals who leverage strategic insights and stay attuned to the community dynamics will significantly improve their chances of success. Aspiring YouTube creators are encouraged to view challenges as opportunities for growth, transforming setbacks into lessons that shape their unique journeys. By embracing these principles outlined in this essay, both novice and experienced creators can master the art of content creation and achieve a thriving presence on the platform, inspiring future generations along the way.

RECAP OF KEY STRATEGIES

In the ever-evolving landscape of YouTube content creation, understanding and leveraging audience engagement is paramount. Successful creators emphasize authentic interactions with their viewers, fostering a community that feels invested in the content. This relationship is cultivated through consistent communication, such as responding to comments and soliciting feedback for future videos. By prioritizing viewer input, creators can tailor their content to what resonates most, ultimately boosting viewer retention and encouraging subscribers to become active participants in the channels growth. Strategies like hosting live Q&A sessions or creating polls can further enhance this connection, making the audience feel valued and appreciated, which in turn can transform casual viewers into loyal followers.

Equally important is the strategic use of video optimization to ensure greater visibility in a saturated market. Creators must familiarize themselves with YouTube's intricate algorithms, focusing on relevant keywords, engaging thumbnails, and compelling titles that accurately represent their content. The value of metadata cannot be underestimated, as it allows videos to rank higher in search results, making it easier for potential subscribers to discover the channel. Leveraging analytics tools provides insight into viewer behavior, enabling creators to make data-informed decisions regarding content style, posting frequency, and topic selection. This analytical approach not only aids in understanding what works but also allows for the identification of emerging trends, fostering a proactive strategy that keeps the channel relevant and engaging.

Social media serves as a powerful ally in driving traffic to YouTube channels. By cross-promoting content on platforms like Instagram, TikTok, and Twitter, creators can tap into diverse audiences, drawing them back to their main channel. Consistency across these platforms amplifies brand recognition and enhances overall engagement. Adaptability is crucial in a rapidly changing digital environment; creators should be prepared to pivot their strategies in response to new trends or platform updates. Adhering to these core strategies—audience engagement, video optimization, and social media utilization—creates a holistic approach for aspiring YouTubers, offering a structured pathway to transforming a fledgling channel into a thriving, subscriber-rich presence.

ENCOURAGEMENT FOR ASPIRING CREATORS

Embarking on the journey of content creation can often feel overwhelming, particularly when faced with the vastness of platforms like YouTube. Many aspiring creators grapple with self-doubt and the intimidating presence of more established influencers. The beauty of this digital age is the democratization of content; anyone with a smartphone and a vision can carve out a niche. Embracing the learning curve inherent in this process is crucial. Each video offers a unique opportunity for growth, both in terms of skill and audience engagement. Remember that every successful creator started where you are now—experimenting, learning from feedback, and refining their craft over time. Celebrate small victories along the way, as they build the foundation for greater accomplishments in the future. The significance of community among creators cannot be understated. Networking with fellow content creators fosters an environment of sharing and support, where ideas can flourish. Engaging with others in the same boat can also alleviate feelings of isolation that often accompany the creative journey. Platforms such as YouTube and social media allow creators to connect, share strategies, and offer constructive feedback. Joining online forums or local meetups can also provide insights that propel you forward. By surrounding yourself with a supportive network, you can gather inspiration and motivation to persevere through challenges. Developing these relationships not only enhances your personal growth but can lead to collaborative opportunities that broaden your audience and amplify your message. Maintaining a consistent and adaptable approach is vital for long-term success in the ever-evolving landscape of YouTube. Algorithms change, audience preferences shift, and trends emerge, demanding a keen awareness of the platforms dynamics. Aspiring creators should commit to regular content production while remaining open to experimentation. Analyze the performance of your videos, utilizing data analytics to refine your strategy and understand what resonates with your audience. This iterative process of creation, analysis, and adjustment will not only enhance your content but also build resilience in the face of setbacks. Remember, the path to millions of subscribers is not linear; it requires perseverance, creativity, and a willingness to evolve continuously. By embracing this journey and remaining steadfast in your passion, success is attainable, and every step taken is a building block toward your ultimate goal.

FINAL THOUGHTS ON YOUTUBE SUCCESS

Success on YouTube requires an intricate blend of creativity, consistency, and strategic planning. Emphasizing the importance of personal branding, creators must establish a unique identity that resonates with their audience. This process starts with recognizing target demographics and tailoring content to meet those audiences preferences and needs. As content creators forge their identities, they should also invest time in community engagement, responding to comments and fostering a sense of belonging among viewers. Such interactive relationships not only enhance viewer loyalty but also encourage word-of-mouth promotion, which can be invaluable for growth. Consistently delivering quality content that reflects the creators brand strengthens viewer trust and retention, ultimately leading to sustained subscriber growth and engagement.

Equally paramount is the understanding and leveraging of YouTube's algorithm, which heavily influences visibility and reach. Aspirants to YouTube success should prioritize keyword research and SEO optimization to ensure their videos are discoverable. This includes crafting compelling titles, engaging thumbnails, and precise tags that align with trending topics and search terms. Analyzing metrics such as watch time, audience retention, and click-through rates can provide critical insights into what types of content resonate most effectively with viewers. Creators should consider experimenting with various formats, lengths, and topics based on these analytics to fine-tune their content strategy. As trends evolve, adaptability becomes a vital component, allowing creators to pivot and refresh their approach in response to new efforts or shifts in viewer preferences. Fostering success on YouTube transcends merely generating content; it encompasses a mindset of continuous learning and innovation. Embracing the inevitability of challenges, whether related to algorithm changes, content saturation, or criticism, is essential for long-term resilience. It involves cultivating a growth-oriented approach that values feedback and experimentation. Networking with other creators can also augment ones reach and introduce fresh ideas that propel a channel forward. By maintaining focus on both quality and the emotional connection with audiences, creators can carve out meaningful niches in the vast ocean of digital content. As this essay outlines, the multifaceted journey to YouTube success—rooted in strategy, community engagement, and adaptability—offers an inspiring roadmap for aspiring creators looking to rise from obscurity to prominence.

CALL TO ACTION FOR CONTINUED LEARNING

The journey to becoming a successful content creator on YouTube extends far beyond initial uploads; it requires a commitment to continuous learning and adaptation. As the platform evolves, so do the strategies that yield success, necessitating a proactive approach to acquiring new skills and insights. Engaging with the plethora of available resources—from online courses and industry podcasts to webinars and creator communities—can significantly enhance ones understanding of effective content creation. This proactive engagement equips creators with up-to-date knowledge about algorithms, audience preferences, and technical skills. By immersing themselves in a culture of continual learning, aspiring YouTubers not only keep their content fresh and relevant but also position themselves to anticipate industry shifts, ensuring sustained growth and relevance in an increasingly competitive landscape.

Actively seeking feedback and participating in peer review can illuminate blind spots that creators may overlook in their self-assessments. This collaborative spirit fosters an atmosphere where ideas can flourish and evolve through constructive criticism. Formulating connections with other creators can lead to collaborations that broaden reach and expose audiences to diverse content. Recognizing and analyzing successful channels within ones niche allows for a more nuanced understanding of what resonates with viewers, prompting creators to refine their approaches. Engaging with an analytical mindset proves invaluable as it empowers creators to iterate on their strategies, facilitating both personal and professional growth as they navigate the multifaceted YouTube ecosystem.

The commitment to ongoing education should embody the mindset of a lifelong learner, allowing creators to remain agile in a fast-paced digital environment. The unique challenges of carving out a niche on YouTube can feel overwhelming, but embracing change and leaning into the learning process can catalyze personal growth and professional success. By creating a habit of self-improvement—whether through winding paths of trial and error or in-depth study—content creators can not only enhance their craft but also cultivate a loyal audience that appreciates their evolution over time. The call to action is clear: seize the opportunities for growth, invest in education, and become a beacon of adaptation and resilience in the dynamic world of YouTube.

BIBLIOGRAPHY

Brian Belland. 'The Role of Criticism in Understanding Problem Solving.' Honoring the Work of John C. Belland, Samuel Fee, Springer New York, 5/27/2012

Ash Blodgett. 'Learning YouTube Analytics.' LinkedIn, 1/1/2020

Jorge Sergers. 'Analysis Techniques for Racecar Data Acquisition.' SAE International, 2/24/2014

Bruce C. Brown. 'The Ultimate Guide to Search Engine Marketing.' Pay Per Click Advertising Secrets Revealed, Atlantic Publishing Company, 1/1/2007

, empreender. 'Social Media Marketing Made Simple.' Editora Bibliomundi, 12/16/2021

Greg Jarboe. 'YouTube and Video Marketing.' An Hour a Day, John Wiley & Sons, 10/7/2011

Simon Lennane. 'Creating Community Health.' Interventions for Sustainable Healthcare, Taylor & Francis, 5/5/2023

Andrea Kupfer Schneider. 'Effective Responses to Offensive Comments.' SSRN, 1/1/2008

Carolyn Jenkins. '7 Seconds to Connect.' 3 Steps to Engage Your Audience with Confidence, Speak with Heart, 8/18/2020

John Schwenkler. 'Anscombe's Intention.' A Guide, Oxford University Press, 10/2/2019

MAX EDITORIAL. 'Amazon KDP Keywords Guide: How to Choose the Best Keywords.' Max Editorial, 9/18/2024

Social Media ProCoders. 'YouTube SEO Mastery: Optimizing Your Channel for Search.' by Mocktime Publication, 3/22/2023

Kyle Loudon. 'Mastering Algorithms with C.' Useful Techniques from Sorting to Encryption, "O'Reilly Media, Inc.", 8/5/1999

Rowan Everhart. 'The YouTube Algorithm.' Decoding the Mystery, RWG Publishing, 7/9/2024

Charles E. Leiserson. 'Introduction to Algorithms, third edition.' Thomas H. Cormen, MIT Press, 7/31/2009

Terry C Power. 'Marketing Your Business With YouTube Shorts.' Power Publishing, 5/29/2024

Delano B. Gurley. 'Thinking Of Writing A Book? Here's What You Need To Know.' A Step By Step Guide To Writing A Quality Book That Sells Quickly, The Door 2 Success Publishing , 9/18/2023

F. Scott Fitzgerald. 'The Great Gatsby: A Graphic Novel Adaptation.' Candlewick Press, 2/2/2021

Radana Dvorak. 'SMART Board Interactive Whiteboard For Dummies.' John Wiley & Sons, 10/2/2012

Mason McCuskey. 'Beginning Game Audio Programming.' Premier Press, 1/1/2003

Ashley Kennedy. 'Avid Editing.' A Guide for Beginning and Intermediate Users, Sam Kauffmann, Taylor & Francis, 1/25/2013

Rachel Bastarache Bogan. 'How to Edit Videos That People Want To Watch.' Renegade Digital Post, 7/1/2017

Joseph V. Mascelli. 'The Five C's of Cinematography.' Motion Picture Filming Techniques, Silman-James Press, 1/1/1998

Benjamin Reid Phillips. 'Storyboarding Essentials.' SCAD Creative Essentials (How to Translate Your Story to the Screen for Film, TV, and Other Media), David Harland Rousseau, Clarkson Potter/Ten Speed, 6/25/2013

Gay Gordon-Byrne. 'Buying, Supporting, Maintaining Software and Equipment.' An IT Manager's Guide to Controlling the Product Lifecycle, CRC Press, 6/25/2014

Graham Swainson. 'Basics of Video Production.' Des Lyver, CRC Press, 5/17/1999

Martin A. Sokoloff. 'Speaking Clearly.' Improving Voice and Diction, Sixth Edition, Jeffrey C. Hahner, Waveland Press, 1/16/2013

Gareth Hardy. 'Smashing Logo Design.' The Art of Creating Visual Identities, John Wiley & Sons, 5/12/2011

David Wisnom. 'Before the Brand.' Creating the Unique DNA of an Enduring Brand Identity, Alycia Perry, McGraw Hill Professional, 1/1/2003

Rachel Gogos. 'Build Your Personal Brand.' The Definitive Guide to Soul-Based Marketing, Amazon Digital Services LLC - Kdp, 12/12/2018

Angela Crocker. 'The Content Planner.' A Complete Guide to Organize and Share Your Ideas Online, Self-Counsel Press, a division of International Self-Counsel Press Limited, 1/1/2017

United States. Department of Defense. Office of the Director of Administration and Management. 'DoD Forms Management Program.' Procedures Manual, Director of Administration and Management, Department of Defense, 1/1/1995

Newt Barrett. 'Get Content Get Customers: Turn Prospects into Buyers with Content Marketing.' Joe Pulizzi, McGraw Hill Professional, 5/2/2009

Moriah Elizabeth. 'Create This Book.' Creative Outlet, 5/17/2015

Theresa Go. 'YouTube Channels For Dummies.' Rob Ciampa, John Wiley & Sons, 9/1/2020

Lauralan Michael. 'Choosing Profitable Niches.' Easy Guide to the First Steps, Independently Published, 11/4/2018

Leo Fitzpatrick. 'How YOU Can Become a Famous YouTuber In 2019.' Use the Newest Strategies in Social Media and Digital Marketing and Facebook Advertising to Explode Your Personal Brand and YouTube Channel Is 2019, Amazon Digital Services LLC - KDP Print US, 3/2/2019

Lewis Dartnell. 'Origins.' How Earth's History Shaped Human History, Basic Books, 5/14/2019

Richard Saul Wurman. 'UnderstandingUnderstanding.' Richard Saul Wurman & Jack Dangermond publication, 1/1/2017

Phillip C. Shon. 'Plan Your Essay.' SAGE, 6/24/2019

Derral Eves. 'The YouTube Formula.' How Anyone Can Unlock the Algorithm to Drive Views, Build an Audience, and Grow Revenue, John Wiley & Sons, 2/24/2021

Kelly J Mays. 'The Norton Introduction to Literature.' Twelfth Edition, W. W. Norton & Company, 10/8/2015

www.ingramcontent.com/pod-product-compliance
Lightning Source LLC
Chambersburg PA
CBHW052254220526
45471CB00001B/330